A Life of Healing

Written and compiled by

Marilyn Preston Evans

Illustrated by

Nick Enderby

Wilberforce Publishing

ISBN   0-9549763-0-4

First published by Wilberforce Publishing 2005

British Library Cataloguing in Publication Data. A catalogue record for this book is available from the British Library.

Wilberforce Publishing

Published by Wilberforce Publishing, 208 Send Road, Send, Woking, Surrey, GU23 7EN

Printed by Arrow Offset, Padmores Yard, St. Johns Mews, St. Johns, Woking, Surrey, GU21 1ZE

IN MEMORY OF

HENRY

TO ALL THE ANIMAL KINGDOM
LET US EXPRESS -

Recognition of their right to be here;

Respect for their estate;

Gratitude for their contribution;

Compassion for their vulnerability;

Healing for their wounds;

Love for their Divinity.

M.C.

CONTENTS

Foreword

I met Marilyn when I interviewed her for my first book, '*Animals are Equal*' and this led to many referrals to her of animals in need of healing, one of whom was Henry, a beautiful cat in whose memory this memoir is being published.

Having been brought up with the idea that spiritual healing was a natural occurrence, I have always turned to healers and have been greatly helped, but there appeared not to be so many healers prepared to devote themselves especially to animals. They are, however, much needed.

Some "healers" are not even vegetarian, which seems to be a great contradiction. The healer, as a channel, has to constantly seek purification in thought, word and deed. The first step is true compassion and that cannot abide the imposition of suffering upon living creatures; to eat them is to degrade mind, body and spirit and this, one who calls him or herself a healer, cannot afford to do. Compassion towards all living things is the very first vital step.

So it was heartening to find someone who was prepared to devote herself almost entirely to the creatures who came to live and be in her care, as well as those who were brought to visit or were to be helped at a distance, either by telephone or letter. Marilyn's healing gift was always available, no matter what was happening in her life; she actually physically cared for some of those creatures in need as well. I have experienced healing myself many times both receiving and giving it. Sometimes it works instantly; sometimes it takes time. Sometimes it appears not to work, but what is sure, is that apparent miracles do happen, all the time and we owe it to the animals to allow them to be helped in this wonderful way.

When we open our minds to animals and enable them to communicate with us, we realise just how much humans so often fail them. I know that Marilyn, as I have done, experienced the pain of this realisation. The anecdotes she has compiled from her healing experiences in this memoir lift the mind to the wondrous possibilities open to us and to them.

1

Those who have known and experienced her work and all of us who have received her newsletters, so assiduously compiled to share information, will have here a reminder of what has been, is and can be. Hearts will surely open and sing at this prospect... even greater things are yet to come. The stories are related in Marilyn's familiar, chatty style, just as if you were in her homely sitting room listening to her recounting the memories of the creatures who have come her way, all individuals, just as much as the human healees were.

Animals are much more than we ever dream of. To open our hearts and minds to this, is to begin upon the path of higher understanding. These stories leave the reader with many questions – it is these which beckon us onwards to greater awareness.

Some of my companion animals have appeared to me after their passing, just as Marilyn describes the appearance of some of hers and the love, beauty and friendship conveyed is pure joy. I also have Marilyn to thank for the introduction of the invaluable Bach Flower Remedies into my life. She very generously gave me a complete set of stock bottles and I have used them for humans, animals and plants ever since. At one period, she became extremely attuned to them with happy results.

These pages will hopefully inspire others to explore the possibilities open to all who have the heartfelt desire to help the light shine brighter for all and everything. Caring and heightened sensitivity does take its toll. Marilyn never stinted on giving of herself and of the healing gift she was given. Surely she will earn that greatest of accolades that any of us could ever hope for from the Father – Mother, "Well done, my good and faithful servant, well done."

Rebecca Hughes Hall

In the Beginning…

My parents owned a grocery and provisions shop on Plymouth Hoe, in Windsor Lane situated directly down from the War Memorial. There I was born, over the shop, in 1933, joining my brother who had arrived three years before me.

Also sharing the three rooms over the shop were a dear old couple, Mr & Mrs Quick, who shared in my upbringing whilst my parents worked extremely hard in the business.

From a very early age my great love was the Animal Kingdom and pet mice became my great interest and intrigue.

George was also a great favourite - he was our tortoise and lived happily in the garden, hibernating in a box of straw during the cold winter months. As we 'played' together I used to tie a small piece of wood or something on his back, wait for him to move to another part of the garden, then 'unload' the little chap, always thinking he enjoyed the game as much as I did. He was probably thinking 'Oh Lord - here we go again!'

Then of course there was dear old Kitty the cat who lived on anything and everything which was left over, as cats and dogs did in those days.

Little did we know that they would soon be in another world…

Thinking of our Kitty reminded me of an article I read in the Sunday Mail supplement a few years ago of another Kitty whose life story was told together with a photograph of her with her 'owner'. Kitty, who lived in the village of Croxton, Staffordshire, had had some two hundred kittens and at the time the photograph was taken, was thirty years old and had just given birth to a further four kittens! She was reckoned to be the oldest living cat in Britain at the time, the previous record was for a twenty eight year old cat.

At the age of six a bad bout of scarlet fever put me in the isolation ward of the Fever Hospital. My parents and Mr & Mrs Quick were only allowed to look in through the huge glass windows separating the wards and the outside world. It seemed like a lifetime in there, alone entirely except for the nurses who came with food, drink and the necessary washing equipment, to each child in their individual 'glass rooms'.

Oh! How glad I was to get home again!

My school reports were full of 'A's- not for grades but for "Absent through illness".

Bobby Horrell's garden backed onto ours at the rear of the shop and we were planning to elope. He came from a large family and all the youngsters had been evacuated, but the situation became too painful for them all to be separated from each other and they were brought back from their various temporary homes to be together again.

The following night the largest explosive to yet hit Plymouth fell from an enemy bomber. They said later it was a two thousand pound landmine. All eight members of Bobby's family were killed apart from a sister whose back was broken. His father's body was found in a tree on the Hoe, so great was the blast. Our home was destroyed and we were all very fortunate to escape with our lives. My parents were saved when their bed was up-ended as it went through the floor trapping them underneath it as the rubble piled up over it. No warning sirens to go to the shelter were sounded.

My young friend was no more. We were just eight years old but the loss was very deep and profound. Where had he gone? Why couldn't I see him again and where were George and Kitty? Nobody could or would give me any answers. It was the fourth of July - American Independence Day 1941.

The following months were a blur going from place to place and for our parents and Mr & Mrs Quick it must have been a nightmare. As a youngster one does not have the responsibilities or the understanding of an adult but we all feared the great fear when the sirens sounded.

For some days following the bombing my mother set up a rescued table in Windsor Lane or what was left of it, and as various tins and goods were dug up from the ruins of our shop she sold them to people who still needed to buy provisions - Our 'Provisions Store' was still in business!

Lady Nancy Astor who lived nearby on the Hoe and who was a customer of ours came to see the devastation and congratulated our mother on her ability and courage to keep going. She had to! Our father was working as a shipwright at Millbay Docks and being bombed out was no excuse not to keep up the war work and keep nose to the grindstone.

It is only on looking back one can appreciate the awful times our elders went through, and still kept going despite the state of things. They were very brave souls and we can be proud of them.

However it was appalling to see others who combed the wrecked homes for everything of any value they could lay their hands on and taking it away in wheelbarrows

Eventually my parents found a flat in Windsor Terrace facing immediately on to the Hoe and it was there on the front room table I had my adenoids removed by our doctor, held down and put under with chloroform - yuk!

Mr and Mrs Quick were lucky to find a small flat in Sussex Place, just along the road from the ruins of our shop and I shared my life between the two homes.

My parents, Kath and Phil, had the shop rebuilt and Mum continued the business from there. Because it stood alone amidst flattened houses it was a target for burglars and we were burgled some eight times which was a tremendous loss each time.

Living next to our flat in Windsor Terrace were Canadian servicemen who kept rabbits in their back garden. When I learned they were fattening them up for the table I was appalled and begged them to let me have them as pets.

They finally gave in and the two beautiful Flemish Giants, a buck and a doe, became mine. Dad built a lovely large hutch for each of them and they were able to have a good free run in the garden each day

One day a terrible storm came and a huge crack of thunder followed a flash of lightning - very close! I raced out of the shop to check on Popsy and Dewey and was devastated to find the doe flat on her side in her hutch, which was covered with a sheet of corrugated galvanised iron to protect the structure. She was dead, apparently struck by lightning.

In a state of shock I picked up her body and draped it over my arm as though there were no bones left in it. Carrying her into the shop I was heartbroken at the death of my little friend. Dad was home from work and helping Mum in the shop and he tried to comfort me saying he would bury her in the garden later on.

But I could not face death again and convincing myself she was not dead I ran up to the garden of our flat just up the back lane with her completely limp body in my arms, breaking my heart.

Laying Dewey out on the grass I hurriedly made a soft bed for her on an old towel and fixed up a temporary home for her in an old cupboard which had been standing in the garden for ages. I managed to find a little dropper, warmed some milk and dropped some drops into the side of her mouth as she lay deadly still on her side on the bed. Nothing stirred. The milk ran out the other side and soaked into the towel.

Throughout the rest of the day and evening I continued to do this despite everyone saying she was dead and must be buried. Early next morning I was straight down in the garden, undid the front covering the temporary hutch and started the ritual all over again. She could NOT be dead! Changing the old towel for some other old material I made the inert body as comfortable as I thought it could be, on the other side this time, and 'fed' her throughout the day. I think everyone thought I was deranged by this time.

Next day the same procedure continued. Then suddenly, in the afternoon, whilst dropping the milk drops in

6

the side of Dewey's mouth there was a TWITCH OF A WHISKER! DEWEY WASN'T DEAD!

An ear moved, a paw flicked, then her beautiful little nose twitched! After that, with renewed heart, I watched as she gradually gathered strength, eating dandelion leaves, grass and all her favourite foods. Later, when she was fit and well she romped with old Pop in the garden behind the shop and a while later there were some beautiful little Pop-Deweys running

round also!

One day a golden coloured dog turned up on the shop doorstep. He had a collar on with a tag showing the name 'Cozey'. We searched in vain for the owner and he somehow attached himself to us.

Whenever my mother had to go down to her parent's home near Mousehole, Dad would take over the shop on his own. Cozey would disappear on the same day and reappear on the day Mum returned. Where he went or how he knew when she was coming back we never did discover, it was quite uncanny. A couple of years later he did not return and we often wondered what had happened to him.

We had a piano accordion in those days and I used to pick out a little tune on it now and again. I'm not sure if anyone ever recognised the tune but Cozey would fling his head back and howl until I stopped. We were never sure if he was joining in or trying to drown it out!

Where Smokey the black cat came from we have no idea but arrive he did and stayed for many years. By this time we had moved to St.Budeaux in Plymouth. My parents continued to run the shop on the Hoe travelling to and fro each

7

day, and Smokey of course remained at home. He was a beautiful cat and much loved by us all. He became ill with a chest infection and the vet took him away to treat him but then sadly told us dear Smokey had died.

Time moves on, and things change…

Motor Bikes!

After passing the eleven plus I left St Andrews Primary School for Stoke Damerel High School for Girls but as the latter school was still being used by the Forces we were accommodated for the first year at Plymouth High School for Girls together with some girls from Devonport High. Others from these schools had opted to go elsewhere until everyone could attend their own school.

After the first year we were all in our rightful places and continued our studies. Our playground was on the roof - four storeys high! Discipline was quite strict in those days. We stood when a mistress walked into the room and we sat only when told to do so. In school uniform we had to behave ourselves or there would be trouble! At all times we had to be properly dressed and no-one ate in the street or on the bus. Homework had to be well written and passed in on time next morning. I did not find the work easy by any means.

Leaving school at sixteen my parents paid for a year's study at Pryor's Academy learning shorthand and typing. I remember well the wooden boards being placed over the keyboard as we read the exercises from our left, woe betide any of us if we slid down in our chairs to peek under the board to see where the letters were! A rap on the knuckles with a ruler, several times, soon got us out of the habit and gradually we improved until our fingers knew where the keys were - more or less.

At seventeen I got my first job, with the Great Western Railway at the old Millbay Station as a shorthand typist. Meantime my brother bought a 350cc Triumph Speed Twin motor bike. One day I borrowed it and drove it around until I found to my horror that I was too short at five feet nothing, to stop it unless I found a high enough pavement edge to put my foot on, without the bike toppling over on me. Coming down the road, where building was in progress on new houses, I hit the wet mud, put on the brakes making the bike go into a spin before it fell over and started careering down the road, with me hanging on like grim death not daring to let go of my brother's beloved bike, he would kill me if

anything happened to it and I can't say I'd blame him!.
Hanging on to the handlebars for dear life we slid relentlessly
down the wet road when suddenly everything went into slow
motion. It's a strange experience, the houses were very, very
slowly passing by as I felt I could stop if I wanted to - or do
anything, actually, time seemed almost to stand still and
everything was absolutely quiet.

We came to a stop almost outside our house, the bike
on its side both wheels now leading, I hanging on fully
stretched out behind it. Gradually getting up, with my brother
racing out of the house, I found my clothes worn away to my
skin which was horribly grazed and my back was hurting!
The result was being in a plaster jacket for six months,
then a spinal steel backed corset for two years. I was told it
could be for several years, but discarded it after two. Today
some sixty years later the effects are still with me and pain in
my back and neck are at times pretty intense.
I met Dennis when I bought my own motorcycle
through him and his firm, and after a meeting with him and a
few of his friends the Plymouth Motorcycle Touring Club was
born. I was the only girl with my own motorcycle and it led
me a pretty dance! It was only a 125cc Royal Enfield, 'The
Flying Flea', the last of the hand change models it had a mind
of its own but it got me to work - most of the time. Very often

on putting it into bottom gear it would suddenly charge backwards and I would crash into something, like the garden fence at home which eventually gave in and fell down after being hit once too often. Being a two stroke I found this could be one of their little problems, the timing would change making the bike go into reverse.

Another fault it had was the twist grip to rev up, constantly slid closed when my hand was taken off for a few seconds i.e. putting my hand out to turn right. Hence I had to dart my hand out and quickly return it to keep the twist grip open to keep the engine going, otherwise the motorcycle would stop halfway round a turn in the road, not altogether satisfactory for other road users. Getting up any speed was dangerous, the windshield would slide down towards my face and I had to keep it up with my chin until I could tighten the nut and bolt holding it in place. I never did get it sorted properly! Oh! - and yes, there was the seat. A spring would often prise itself loose and cause untold discomfort until I could stop somewhere, find the screwdriver and put it back into a safe position again. All in all one could call it a death trap but as I said it usually got me to work more or less on time.

However, came the day when I nearly didn't get home again! We left the offices at Millbay Station with a flourish on Friday afternoons before the train came in to stop at the buffers for its week-end cleaning. I put on my 'crash helmet' which was actually an old RAF leather flying helmet, scarf, coat and gloves, loaded my things into the carrier, sat astride the Enfield a few feet away from the edge of the platform and noted the train was coming into the station. But I would be well away and out under the stone arches before it actually arrived, so I kick-started and put her into bottom gear revving up nicely. Letting out the clutch we were away, BACKWARDS!

Suddenly I found the rear wheel spinning over the railway track with me straddling the bike, both feet on the very edge of the platform, with the train steaming straight for the buffers a few short yards from us! HELP! It was impossible to get off and impossible to let go! Thankfully two

11

porters were close by and came rushing to pull the bike and me safely out of the way in the nick of time. The Flying Flea and I parted company soon after that.

Dennis and I went to see a film one evening and I felt unwell with terrible stomach pains, having to be carried out and taken to see our doctor as an emergency. He decided I had indigestion and sent me home with some tablets for the condition.

Next morning, a Sunday, my parents called an ambulance and at six-thirty I was rushed into hospital with a burst appendix and a huge ovarian cyst. I didn't know much more until the following afternoon, when I heard that all the family had gone off on a picnic, with me dying in a hospital bed! How could they? Then peritonitis set in and another operation was necessary.

Eventually I returned home and my parents cared for me but I felt very, very ill. Something was very wrong. Pus was coming from the operation scar and I had to return to hospital where yet another operation found a swab had been left in causing complications. Things took a long time to heal and the adhesions took several years to stop paining me. I was not a comfortable person.

Marriage

Dennis and I were married in February 1957. We both had medical check-ups and I was informed that due to my medical history it was doubtful if we could have children, we were extremely disappointed, naturally.

However, soon afterwards I found I was pregnant and we looked forward to the great event. The morning sickness every day was appalling and I used to travel to work on the train in the guard's van, holding a bowl in a shaking hand all the way. On the 26th September at six and a half months pregnant, regular pains came on  whilst at my desk and I was taken to hospital into the very bed in which I'd had my last major surgery! The curtains were pulled around the bed and I was left.

The pains became excruciating and as I waited for help my baby son was born dead. The little body was taken away. Heartbroken, I drifted in and out of sleep. Sometime later, in great pain I was taken to the operating theatre; the afterbirth was causing trouble. Several days had to be spent in hospital. Perhaps the worst part was, having lost my longed for son, the ward leading off ours was Ward 6A where women who had tried to abort their babies had them successfully and the babies were carried, crying, through our ward at various times of the day to be taken to their mothers to be fed. I found that unbelievably cruel, with three of us in Ward 6 just having lost our own babies. On returning home I was in severe trouble with milk fever, no-one had thought to give me anything to stop the production of milk and it was agony for several weeks.

In those days no-one talked about such things as counselling or bereavement.

13

Late the following year, at five and a half months pregnant, my second son was born dead and I went into a deep depression at this further loss. I was later transferred to the local Saltash Hospital, but on the day I was due to return to our home I developed an extremely painful leg and arm. A doctor was sent for and he diagnosed thrombosis - it was explained to me there was a possibility I could die if the clots reached my heart and I was TERRIFIED! The arm and leg were plastered in an awful smelling tarry substance, bound with bandages and then tied straight with boards to stop any movement. Heartbroken, depressed and very frightened, I was in hospital for several weeks before being unbound and allowed home. For some reason I thought if I could hold onto someone living I could not die, so when anyone came within grabbing distance of my bed, I would shoot out my good arm to hang on to them, so terrified was I of dying, while I was in hospital.

Again there was no-one to talk to, and no-one who could understand what I was going through. Everyone kept tight-lipped and again evaded the subject. They thought if they changed the subject and kept cheerful I would 'get over it'. I never found out what happened to our two babies, no-one ever discussed it. But thankfully, I know now that they are both well, happy and fine on another plane of Life and I look forward to meeting up with them again one day.

My mother came to look after me at our home and it was several weeks before I could go out of doors. Even then if I saw someone coming along the road with a pram, I would break down and run home in floods of tears.

Dennis joined the Army Cadet Force and I wrapped my life around our two dogs, Panda, the Old English Sheepdog and Kim, the Collie, both lovely souls and to whom I owe much gratitude for their unconditional love and who saved my sanity. I used to run the canteen for the cadets and because Dennis spent practically every night, weekends and holiday with the Army Cadet Force, the dogs and I used to join the camps, I as 'cook' and the dogs as companions and to have fun with the boys. If you can't beat them, join them, they say!

14

One day a baby robin was brought to me in our little flat which was our home in those days. Hand-rearing Phoebe was a wonderful therapy. She came with us all on the ACF weekend camps, caged at night but flying out during the day, though not far from the tent with her cage. Her photo appeared in The Western Morning News, with her sitting between the paws of Panda, the caption reading *'Panda, the Old English Sheepdog guards pet Robin'* which was very far from the truth. Panda was terrified of Phoebe and had to be bribed to stay sitting there, with her favourite biscuits!

Our doctor suggested we try again for a child, but I could not possibly go through all that again, having to spend six or seven months or so in hospital as was suggested, to 'make sure' everything would be alright! Apart from that I could not bear to be parted from Panda and Kim.

In 1962 we bought this house, on mortgage, and moved in, well I did, with the help of friends carrying all the furniture the few hundred yards down the road. Dennis was away at camp for the week with the ACF boys, where else?!

By this time birds and animals began to arrive for help as more and more people realised that injured and helpless creatures could receive help and sanctuary here. Dennis built aviaries and pens, a flight and a small pool for sea birds - some of which came from the massive Torrey Canyon disaster with the appalling oil spillage. It was a great financial struggle and some friends helped with jumble sales etc. to buy fish for the birds, bless them, and we kept going. The small number of us doing this voluntary rescue work in the South West were not allowed one penny from the millions of pounds poured in by generous people throughout the country. One friend in Cornwall sold all her jewellery, then her furniture for the fish to keep the birds going. We never knew what happened to the surplus millions, but it was desperately traumatic for the poor birds. Standing on the concrete for so long their heels became raw and had to be bound each day, in their unnatural environments. I dread hearing of oil spills and damage to wildlife.

The Voice

In early September 1969 an unknown lady in Devon sent me a bottle of Dr. Edward Bach Flower Remedies of which I'd never heard before. About to throw the contents away, because of the unknown source, I cautiously took the four drops as instructed on the bottle four times daily wondering what it was supposed to do. The short letter accompanying the bottle was kindly and well intended, so I trusted that it was alright to take the contents. At the time an awful cold and sore throat was developing which always lead to a very bad couple of weeks at least.

By the morning following the first day's Remedies, the cold and sore throat had cleared up!!! But that was surely coincidence? By the end of the week I began to feel very different; the tension was gone and I felt relaxed for the first time in ages. What were the magic contents of the bottle?

Writing to my benefactor, I told her what had happened and asked if she could tell me more about these Dr.Bach Remedies. She kindly sent a leaflet about them and told me I was taking the remedy Vervain for tension and stress. Immediately I wrote to the Dr. Bach Centre in Wallingford and became absolutely fascinated with the subject of the thirty-eightremedies and the rescue Remedy, and what they could do for people and animals - and plants! I began to use them with the birds and animals in my care here and they helped a great deal, thankfully.

One Saturday about a week later, I was in the kitchen preparing a ham salad, for Dennis, myself and Ernie Quick, who was living with us then, following the passing of his beloved wife Annie, when suddenly a clear voice spoke to me quite distinctly and forcefully, saying "Lyn, you're a hypocrite! You call yourself an animal lover and yet you eat the corpses of animals and birds. You are eating more than you are helping. YOU WILL NOT COMPLETE THE MISSION YOU CAME TO THE EARTH PLANE TO DO UNTIL YOU STOP EXPLOITING THE ANIMAL KINGDOM."

Oddly enough I was not surprised, I had never heard The Voice before, yet it seemed quite natural and quite familiar. But I was extremely puzzled about the mission??? And the Earth plane - as far as I was aware at that time, this was the only 'plane'.

I argued with The Voice that I liked eating meat and flesh foods, though I could see that it was illogical. Here was I, almost penniless, caring for so many birds and animals being brought in ill, sick and dying, breaking my heart when they died and yet at the same time eating more than I was saving! I told The Voice that even if I stopped eating that sort of food, it would not make any difference as everyone else would still continue to eat it, so it would be pointless. The Voice immediately, before I even finished putting in my piece replied "It is of no concern of yours what others do - do you have to be one of the flock of sheep and do something because others do it? It is what you and what others do according to their own inner and deeper feelings which is so very important to progress and non-progress."

Yes, I could see that too now that it was pointed out to me but I retaliated that it would make no difference if I stopped being involved in eating flesh foods - millions of animals and birds would still be bred, live and die, often in the most brutal and horrific way to be eaten by humans... I was again interrupted with the Voice saying that if I wanted to complete the mission I came to do, then I should not eat my dead friends - for to me, the Animal Kingdom involves my friends. The Voice was silent. My weak remark then was "Well, I don't have to kill them to eat them."

The quick response to that came back - "Then that is even worse- you expect others to do something for your benefit, which you have not the guts to do yourself!" True! I was floored on every count.

The Voice continued - "You have free will to choose - you are not being forced" Silence.

Putting the ham from my plate on to the other two plates I had much food for thought and a horrible sinking feeling in my stomach, what was I going to live on? A meal

17

has the main item, flesh. Then one considers what to put with it, well that was the way I worked out our meals!

Never had I considered going vegetarian, which was not a popular thing way back over thirty five years ago.

But the Voice was kindly, direct and also authoritative. It stated facts and did not mince words. It was obviously very wise and knew much more than I.

That evening we had kippers for tea, and as I was busily immersed in my thoughts about preparing the meal, cutting the bread, dashing around as usual to get things done as quickly as possible, I popped the kippers on the plates, with a helping of baked beans. Suddenly The Voice asked me what I was doing.

"Getting our tea, we're having kippers!"

"Five bodies you have prepared there to eat. Would you kill your goldfish and eat them?" I was aghast at the very idea. "They're my friends!"
"But because you did not know these fish, because you don't consider them your personal friends, you want to eat them?"

It had not crossed my mind about fish and exploiting them with their untimely deaths. I often cried over the animals and birds, the terrible, terrible plight of factory farmed animals and birds and those in vivisection laboratories, zoos, circuses, hunts and such. How would we like to endure what they have to? Have those exploiting the Animal Kingdom no conscience? No pity? No feelings at all? Don't they realise that the creatures feel pain, fear, terror, grief, frustration, hopelessness, anguish in much the same way as we humans? Surely humanity will wake up to these facts one day?

I put the kippers onto the other two plates and thought this was going to be great, what was I going to eat for the rest of my life? Then I cheered myself up with the thought that it may only be another twenty to thirty years.

Next day, twenty to thirty years might as well be three hundred years - it seemed a long time ahead without any of the food I had been used to.

The Sunday lunch was already bought of course - it was to be a nice roast chicken with all the trimmings - lovely! Having prepared the meal and set it on the table for the three

of us, I had the first forkful of delicious chicken almost in my mouth when suddenly The Voice came "How many more times?" Stopping dead in my tracks I mentally asked "Can't I have my last mouthful of chicken?"
"You have the free will to choose which path to follow but remember what I told you yesterday".
Silence.

By this time my husband and Ernie were getting a bit concerned about my behaviour over my meals at this weekend. Was I sickening for something they wanted to know? How could I explain about The Voice? They would have thought me out of my tiny mind. Just saying I did not fancy it any more I proceeded with the other food on my plate.

Two days later I was reading some vegetarian literature from the Health Food shop, when I came, for the first time, upon the subject of veganism. Here were some people living not just as vegetarians, but not having any product of the animal kingdom at all! No milk, butter, eggs, cheese, using no wool or leather, not drinking out of bone china cups, the list was endless of what we use and abuse the animals for, thank goodness then, I was just going to be a vegetarian!

The Voice popped up with "You will have to be one of those people if you are not to exploit the Animal Kingdom" Oh my God, no! I couldn't do it! How could I live like that? But I already knew it had to be even though I still had free will.

From that moment on I had nothing at all from the animal world for the next eight years and whilst at first I found it very difficult, with time it improved and my body no longer wanted the things it normally had. I began to feel very much better in myself and had more energy. It's about the only time I disciplined myself very strictly, but then, I was on a mission! In those eight years I was never ill and felt very fit and active, with very little sleep or spare time whatsoever.

It was only following three terrible personal shocks in three months in 1977 that I fell by the wayside and became just a vegetarian and years later began to eat fish again.

Lychgate - The Entrance to the Path

That same month of September 1969 saw my life and thoughts change dramatically. Following the Vervain remedy, then The Voice and veganism, another major event occurred.

I don't know how I came to be writing to a prisoner in Yorkshire called Ken, who was suffering from cancer. Ken had tried desperately to keep his business going and had 'cooked the books' hoping to straighten things out when the business prospered again. But things went from bad to worse and he was imprisoned and was terribly depressed. As I say, I have no idea how I came to be corresponding with him in prison.

One day Ken sent a book to me with his letter telling me I must read it. Putting off reading the book, eventually Ken insisted I had to set aside everything and READ THE BOOK!

And so it was, on this late September afternoon, with dozens of birds and animals in my little hospital to care for, and using only orthodox treatment and the wonderful vet's help, I sat down, reluctantly to read this little book which Ken insisted I was to read.

Several years before, I had come across vivisection for the first time and what I read shattered me. I just could not believe that humans could be so relentlessly cruel to animals and birds, and the more I read the more desperate I felt. When I became suicidal Dennis threatened to burn the growing amount of literature and books I was studying on the terrible subject. I hated suffering and fear myself and to think of what was being inflicted on the Animal Kingdom was too much to bear.

Joining the National Anti-Vivisection Society I brought into being the Saltash Branch of NAVS and we had several hundred members join in Devon and Cornwall, who all wished to find humane alternatives to experiments on over five and a half million un-anaesthetised animals in this country alone at that time, every year, many of these unfortunate creatures dying appalling and lingering deaths.

Lady Muriel Dowding, founder of Beauty Without Cruelty, and wife of Air Chief Marshal Lord Dowding, leader of the great Battle of Britain who saved our country during World War II, kindly agreed to become our patron and we were greatly honoured.

All through those painful years of trying to 'fight' the cruelties of vivisection I prayed to someone I really did not believe in then, though brought up in a Church of England school with religion thrown down our throats for the first hour of every single school day. I fervently prayed that I could find A BETTER WAY than all this terrible suffering - there must be something better, kinder, somewhere surely? But what? Where? How?

So that September afternoon I picked up Ken's gift of the little book - *Lychgate - Entrance to the Path* by Air Chief Marshal Lord Dowding, Chief of Fighter Command during the Battle of Britain, GCB, GCVO, CMG. (Lord Dowding also wrote the wonderful books *Many Mansions, and The Dark Star.*)

Digressing again I quote from a speech delivered by Lord Dowding in the House of Lords several years ago and after becoming a vegetarian following visits to slaughter houses and after finding out personally some of the atrocities in vivisection laboratories: *".....I firmly believe that painful experiments on animals are morally wrong, and that it is basically immoral to do evil in order that good may come.....All Life is one and all it's manifestations with which we have contact are climbing the ladder of evolution. It is an important part of our responsibilities to help them in their ascent, and not to retard their development by cruel exploitation of their helplessness.*

..Failure to recognise our responsibilities towards the animal kingdom is the cause of many of the calamities which now beset the nations of the world. Nearly all of us have a deep rooted wish for peace - peace on earth; but we shall never attain true peace.. until we recognise the place of animals in the scheme of things and treat them accordingly."

Brave words by a very brave soul! But then again if it had not been for his foresight and determination during the Battle of Britain, Britain might well not be the free country that it is today.But back to the book - Lychgate!

21

The more I read, the more deeply intrigued I became in Lord Dowding's words. He explained most clearly that THERE WAS NO DEATH! No-one and nothing can really die! We all move out of our physical bodies but we, the 'Eternal We', cannot die. That came as a most wonderful revelation. My two sons were not dead! Mrs Quick was not dead! Bobby Horrell was not dead! All my beloved birds and animals were not dead! We all live on and as love is the link this draws us together again. We can still communicate with our loved ones! He himself was in contact with hundreds of 'his Boys' - those young RAF lads who 'died' fighting to save our country. He passed on hundreds of messages to bereaved parents from their sons and to wives from their husbands. Messages which uplifted and gave hope to those grieving their terrible losses. Working behind the scenes Lord Dowding was a tower of strength and hope when all seemed lost to so many.

Getting over that wonderful news, I carried on reading that afternoon until I felt as though I had been struck by lightening!

Here the great man was telling me that God could use thousands of people as channels for healing! THAT WAS IT! Throwing the book down on the table in our front room, alone in the house, I stood up, arms upstretched and shouted aloud "I CAN DO THAT - WHY DIDN'T YOU TELL ME THAT BEFORE?".

Racing up into the garden, I took the blind Dutch rabbit out of his hutch, put him on the low flat wall beside it and held my hands over his shaking body, mentally asking God to please heal him. He had been brought in weeks ago, blind, with scars over both eyes unable to close his eyelids, ears flat down, shaking with pain and fear. The vets had done all they could for the poor creature but eventually we decided between us that it was cruel to keep him alive in that condition and it would be kinder to put him out of his misery. Each day I would take him out of the hutch put him on the grass and he would slowly crawl around in a little circle, shaking all the while, until put back in the hutch again where he would sit and tremble. I had to hand feed him as he was not able to see his food and water. It was no life for a rabbit. Some rabbits are forced into these conditions in laboratories and have to endure their lives like this, often just for beauty products! Or testing soap.

Putting him back into his hutch I asked God or whoever it was God had chosen to help him, to please heal him and take care of this poor little rabbit. I gave him some food and water and covered the front of the hutch as normal. On Saturday morning the vet was coming to put him to sleep.

Susie the hen was in a dreadful state too. She had gapeworm very badly and in trying to eject these from her windpipe had battered her head on the garden wall until it was swollen out of all proportion and she could not see. Practically all the feathering was gone from her head and neck. The vets again had done all they could to kill the gapeworms but they persisted in their torment of the bird making her life unbearable. I had to keep her in a large padded box to save further injury. The vet was to put Susie to sleep on the Saturday morning also.

It was getting dark by this time and I could only clean Susie's box as usual, give her her food and drink and close up the padded box for the night in one of the aviaries.

Next morning I went up into the garden early, unfurled the rabbit's hutch and lo and behold there was a bright eyed bushy tailed rabbit, eyes clear as a bell with no sign of scarring, ears pricked up and awaiting a real run in the garden! YES! THIS WAS HEALING! This was how it should be - no cruelty to any other creature, but all done gently and kindly by a Power far greater than we can understand. Putting him out into the garden he raced away, leaping up with bounds of excitement and happiness. And I felt as happy as he did - and so very humble that I broke down and wept with gratitude.

Going into the aviary on this Friday morning I took Susie out of her box sat her on the wall and again mentally asked for healing help for her as she sat quietly clucking for quite a while. Setting her down on the grass she did not move as I cleaned out her quarters, fed and watered her and put her back in the box. Then it was time for the rabbit to go back into his hutch for his own food and water and for the feeding and cleaning out of all the other birds and animals under my care.

In the evening I did the same again with Susie the hen and then put her back in her padded box for the night.

The next morning Dennis went up into the garden first and came down saying "What's up with Susie?"
"Oh God - what's happened now?"
"Well, there was no banging from the box, with her head, so I opened it up and I think you had better go up and have a look."

I raced up expecting the worst but there was Susie out in the aviary strutting around picking up bits and pieces, no shaking of the head, which had gone down almost to its normal size and looking as bright as she could be! Oh, this was absolutely WONDERFUL! A SECOND MIRACLE! I had never heard of healing before the previous day and yet here it was happening in my very own back garden among my beloved creatures! Putting her out in the garden, I took the rabbit out of the hutch and it was truly remarkable and humbling to see them both healed and happy.

We could not afford a telephone in those days, of course, so I hurried down to the town to telephone the vet and cancel the visit with vastly uplifted heart and mind.

With an introduction to healing like that how could one not believe in miracles and what else could happen in the future here with birds and animals?

The debt of gratitude to Lord Dowding is beyond price and I was so grateful to Ken who in his prison, had wanted so much to help me by receiving *Lychgate - The Entrance to the Path.*

That was the beginning of many, many miracles both with animals and humans over some thirty years, just a few of which are recorded here. I only wish it could be said that all were healed but unfortunately this was not the case. Some took a long time to get better, some were not healed at all. I was never to understand who could respond and who could not. People later came with their animals from far and near for healing, and for themselves very often. Folk would write for absent healing and it was quite amazing how we saw this 'working' at great distances - even to Australia - but again not always...

Air Chief Marshal Lord Dowding

It was shortly after this that, I received an invitation to spend the weekend with Air Chief Marshal Lord and Lady Dowding at their beautiful home at Calverley Park in Tunbridge Wells.

Lady Dowding kindly met me at the station. On arrival I was shown over their home, introduced to the secretaries and then taken to see Lord Dowding. I was wondering what I was doing in such grand company and what to do at the meeting with this great man. However, on entering the room, he greeted me with "Ah - the young lady from Cornwall with the birds and animals!" and held out a welcoming hand. Taking it, I felt I was with a favourite grandfather, and was immediately at ease and extremely comfortable in his company. We talked about life after death, reincarnation, karma, vegetarianism, animal welfare and vivisection, and he kindly signed my treasured copy of "*Lychgate*".

Lady Dowding's sister, Kathleen (known as Tottie), then joined us, together with their mother, Mrs. Farrant and their lovely little fourteen year old dog.

Lord and Lady Dowding both remembered fragments of past lives. Many years before they physically met and married, Hugh had appeared to Muriel and sat on the end of her bed and spoken with her about this event in the future. They immediately recognised each other when they eventually physically met.

Another houseguest at the time was Jon Evans, a homeopath, herbalist and psychologist. Lady Dowding, Kathleen and I attended his lecture later that evening in Tunbridge Wells, which was extremely interesting. He was treating several cancer patients with mistletoe at the time, with excellent results.

We returned for supper, having previously enjoyed a sumptuous vegetarian meal overlooking the beautiful Calverley Park and a most fascinating discussion in what we found to be our common ground.

Their little dog, Timmy, was tucking into his meal - a special dish on a serviette on the floor, each section of the dish containing vegetarian foods of various kinds. He cleared each section before starting on the next one!

We talked until about ten-thirty, by which time Lord Dowding, at eighty six years of age, was more than ready for his bed.

Most interesting correspondence ensued and the following year, I think it was, a 'Battle of Britain' card arrived from them saying they were about to see the film again 'with all the Royals - we welcome the Queen on her arrival.' Sir Laurence Olivier played Lord Dowding as Commander-in-Chief of Fighter Command and one of the chief architects of Britain's victory.

I was amazed to see, sometime later, a press article stating 'Few realise that this quiet genius was already in contact with higher realms and receiving and sending communications to them and those people inhabiting them. He takes facts. He examines them carefully. And his sincerity cannot be questioned. Survival after death is his unalterable conviction.'

In all his books, including also *"The Dark Star"*, Lord Dowding imparts spiritual knowledge as he personally had experience of it. He writes of his contact with those on higher levels of consciousness as well as those on lower levels, which he encountered whilst doing 'rescue work'. *"And now call on the Love Ray and send it out over this sad Dark Star, and let the love of the Most High drench and purify every darkest corner of the Earth plane. Let the light from the Holy of Holies shine forth in brilliance. Let fear stumble and die. Let hope rise triumphant. Let hatred fade away in the blinding glory of His everlasting day, and in His keeping may we walk in peace. Amen"*

The knowledge and wisdom, which he shared with me, his reader and listener, was invaluable - priceless. To know that there was no death was a revelation to me in 1969. That loved ones go onto another dimension of life, I was then able to explain it as being like a television set - or nowadays - a computer - where we can all pick up various frequencies.

Our sets receive the signals so that we can see the pictures and messages. These sights and sounds and messages are all around us but because they are on another wavelength or frequency from our normal five senses, we are not aware of them. Any more than we are aware of our loved ones, normally, after they have passed from their physical body, whether human, animal or bird.

I have now seen photographs of people who have passed on, and their loving messages, received on computers and on televisions, as well as reading of others who have 'come through' on radio and audio tape recordings, with their voices. Exciting stuff! I have also read of animals and birds materialising to be with their loved ones again. This has happened also under controlled conditions with scientists present. But why is this not general knowledge and it is only by diligent searching that one comes across such treasures?

Lord Dowding had not been afraid of ridicule or being laughed at for his Truths - he said "Laugh with those who laugh at you. Tell them of the wise man who once said to me - "It's not a bad thing to be a bit cracked - it lets the light in!"

The Blackbird and the Hedgehog

Still in the early days of my healing work with birds and animals, many 'miracles' happened. The instant ones are very lovely, where, as you allow the healing to flow through one can actually see the change for the better taking place. Some cases took a little longer, some a long time. And unfortunately in some cases no change at all was apparent.

In the summer of 1970 a blackbird was brought in by the then Assistant Controller of Plymouth Airport. The bird was in a sad state with a bone from its broken leg protruding out through the feathers at the top of the thigh. My Voice told me to put a Plaster of Paris on the leg, after tractioning the bone back into position.

This I did, tending the patient gently, who was a model of patience and good nature. He simply sat quietly in his 'hospital box', ate his meals, had a drink, and watched the happenings around him. On the third day my Voice telepathically told me to remove the plaster, but by the same method it was applied, i.e. soaked in warm water and the bandage un-wound, which I had never done before, always cutting to remove it. I argued with the instructions saying the leg could not possibly be mended in just three days - it would take three weeks for a simple fracture to mend, let alone a complicated fracture! The Voice insisted the plaster was to be removed. When I did so, lo and behold, the leg was perfectly healed and the blackbird walked proudly round on it with a sparkle in his eyes - and I with much delight in my heart. He was released to the wild a few days later, but not before I had written to the British Veterinary Association about the case

On the 20th June, 1970, I wrote to the B.V.A to ask how long was the minimum period for a blackbird's broken leg to be kept in plaster before being perfectly healed, already aware that this is accepted as three weeks, but needing their written confirmation, about this 'miracle' healing.

The reply from the B.V.A was received on the 24th June, stating the leg should have healed twenty-one days after the plaster was put in position and assuming it was a simple fracture and not a complicated one, such as the bone protruding through the skin.

I replied on the 29th June saying that the blackbird in question was totally healed of a complicated fracture of the leg in just three days, with healing being given and mentally sought for the bird. I had already treated some eight hundred or so birds and animals, using mainly orthodox methods (before knowing about spiritual healing for them in 1969), in the years I had run the little wild bird and animal hospital here. I suggested healing should be investigated more thoroughly and that I had found it could be absolutely miraculous in many cases, quoting some other cases of note. But no reply was ever received as indeed with many a letter I wrote on the subject no-one really wanted to know anything about it unless personal help was needed for someone or their friends, relatives or pets. I feel sure that many people in the medical and veterinary fields are natural healers but are completely unaware of this spiritual gift, unfortunately.

It was grand to see all the wonderful cures happening 'before my very eyes' - but terrible when nothing happened or a little one passed on.

One Sunday morning a hedgehog was brought in, in a really dreadful state. The young couple had found him the day before on the Looe Road in Cornwall. They put him in their car and brought him home to discover the floor of the car crawling with maggots - not a pretty sight! The poor hedgehog's leg wasn't either! The unfortunate little chap had no bone whatsoever in what remained of one of his hind legs, just a flap of skin was holding a lifeless foot; maggots had eaten most of the leg away and part of the intestines, so that when he ate something, the food travelling through him pushed out through the lower intestines. Normally it would have been a completely hopeless case and no veterinary surgeon would have contemplated trying to save him.

But I had already come to find that with healing one is not speaking in normal terms - here we find something far beyond normal, something we would have no idea how it worked or even try to do the things It could do, without any apparent difficulty at all. There is, it seems, no difficulty in the order of the miracles!

Taking the hedgehog in, saying I could promise nothing, but would ask for healing help for him, the young couple told me they had put him in a bucket of water and Dettol to clear out the maggots, then poured iodine onto what was left of the leg, so that, in fact, it looked like a piece of burnt wood hanging out from him, rather than a leg. He was in a shocked state, and I put him into a special heated box and gave him some cat food, with Dr.Edward Bach Flower Remedies - Rescue Remedy for the shock and panic, Gorse for the hopeless state, and Crab Apple to cleanse and purify.

The following day, the television team of Spotlight South West, Plymouth called to film some animal healing for a programme they had already arranged with me here. Bob Deere did the interview and the hedgehog was filmed, with the story of how he had been just brought in the previous day, with very little of his hind leg left. They thought little could be done to help him, but I promised to let them know if a miracle happened.

Two or three days later, the most appalling smell permeated the house as gangrene set in. I had to move the hedgehog and box up into the greenhouse, minus the heating in the box, but continued giving healing and the Dr.Bach Flower Remedies. A tight muslin cover kept further flies out of the box. I knew within myself that God, the Healing Intelligence, this great Power, could still heal the little creature if that was in the Divine Plan for him.

Whenever I say, "**I** gave healing", it should read, "**WE** gave healing", for it is the healer and this 'Something Else' which work together. It is not necessary for anyone to know a healer, I don't think, to receive or ask for help for yourself or someone else, because it is available to everyone

31

and every living thing, as we are all part of this Supreme Intelligence. I believe that we, as humans are no more important to It than an elephant or an ant. We are all Spirit with a different looking overcoat or body, which is left behind when it dies - the real Being which inhabits the body continues to live on. We continued to give the hedgehog his daily requirements, care and healing. And then I was privileged to witness yet another of the growing miracles.

At the end of the third week, our little friend had completely re-grown a perfect leg! It is a very humbling experience to witness and be part of such an event; something which is totally beyond anything medically possible and it did not involve vivisection, experiments and suffering on any other poor creature. It carried no debt of Karma. It just 'happened' through this Greater Power of which each one of us is part and can attune mentally to, within our  own thought structure, deep within where the Real World is known, but mostly forgotten - just a glimpse now and then perhaps, or a second or two when time stands still and one feels at Home and at Peace. Our young patient had re-grown part of the leg bone, muscle, tissue and was perfectly bodied once again.

Here, then, at the end of just three weeks, our hedgehog was renewed and made whole again, running around perfectly fit and well. It was grand to see him and I learned yet another lesson of what can happen through prayer, which is thought, to the Creator - if it is meant to happen.

The Owl & the Pussycat

Another of my early patients was Pip, the baby Tawny Owl who was brought in, in a distressed state and literally starving to death. However, with force-feeding, he survived and began to thrive, taking food readily from my hand, and then from a dish. He got on very well with Bubbles, our Cornish tail-less cat, who had been living under a workmen's hut on a building site. Dennis had an idea, one day, and made up a mock cardboard boat, painting it pea-green, with a 'sail' topped with a five pound note. We made a backdrop from a blue sheet and placed the boat in front of this in the lounge bay. Sitting Bubbles one side of the mast and Pip the other, just looking over the side of the boat, we took a photograph which turned out great.

Some years later, when I was invited to give a talk on healing and UFOs on Radio Devon, with Dave Bassett, the well known radio presenter, I was for some unknown reason impressed to take this photo to the studio with me. David introduced the programme with the song 'The Owl and the Pussycat went to sea in a beautiful pea-green boat'. I was amazed and quickly found the photograph of Pip and Bubbles, holding it up for him to see across the desk., Then it was his turn to be amazed, telling the listeners, when the song finished that he was actually looking at a photo of a live owl and pussycat in a pea-green boat, with a £5 note pinned to the mast!

As we finished the hour long programme, I was talking about UFOs and a little of my own UFO experience in 1971. Just as we ended the session suddenly there was pandemonium. All power had shut down and we were totally off the air. For two whole minutes silence reigned supreme on Radio Devon throughout the whole area of Devon and Cornwall, some parts of Wales and other places - if they're lucky.... David called across the desk for me to put the power back on again - there was little I could do about it, as I had asked our Space friends to make their presence felt in some way or other, to give a bit of back-up please.

But back to Pip now in his aviary again. By now he was about two months old and getting quite noisy at night, having a calling session, throughout the night, with two other owls in a large tree just off the main road. Neighbours began to complain about the noise, whilst I felt more and more guilty until one evening I left the top of the aviary door open for him to fly free if he wanted to do so. Next morning the aviary was open and Pip had 'flown the nest' and was gone. Later that morning I went up the road, to the main road, and began walking the short distance into the town. But as soon as I started along the main road, I heard the most tremendous commotion coming from a large tree in someone's garden. Naturally I stopped to find out what it was all about, and there, half way up a huge tree was little Pip, terrified and being dive bombed by many birds... I knew that it is part of some wild birds' defence tactics against predators to do this, dropping their excrement on the intruder below them until it can become encased and unable to move.

Coming back from shopping in the town the same excited noise came from dozens of angry and upset smaller birds encircling the unfortunate Pip, who was too scared to move. Calling to him, I was hoping that he would come to his name but not a movement occurred.

In the evening I again went to the top of our road and was met by the same scene, I tried the same calling, but not a movement.I returned home a very worried bird -carer.

The following day, the same sight met my eyes, with the raucous sound of the many birds around him and above him, dropping their little parcels on poor Pip in all his innocence

That same night I had a brilliant idea. At that time I was not yet a vegetarian and had a chicken in the fridge, complete with her poor head still on. Cutting the head off, I tied it to the top of a long pole, found the large torch and set off at midnight up the road and onto the main road where I shone the torch on the chicken's head atop the pole and walked up and down the pavement opposite Pip's tree, now silent of bird cries. "Hoo Hoo Hooing" in my best owl's voice, I continued to 'talk' to Pip mentally asking him to come down to me - stupidly thinking he'd know what an unfortunate chicken's head looked like as a food source.

Several cars passed by in the time I did my stint, but none of them stopped - nor did a police car arrive to take me away, as one might think. - nor did Pip stir from his branch high in the tree. But I reckon several people must be wondering to this very day why a woman in Saltash was walking up and down the pavement waving a lit up chicken's head on a pole - I reckon they won't be coming this way again! Oh well - it was worth a try!

By the third day I was extremely worried - something had to be done before the little chap starved to death. But what? I know! The RSPCA! Ringing the Inspector in Cornwall I stated the problem and asked him if he could please help. Unfortunately he said it was not possible.

As we had no telephone, I had telephoned from a friend's house on the main road. She suggested the Army, whom I contacted, asking if they could have a bit of tree-climbing practice to rescue a marooned young owl, but they wouldn't come out to play either. How about the Fire Service? They did not think it was that urgent and were sure Pip would fly off when he really got hungry.

I came home very disappointed and extremely worried about the owl's fate. Why do I always put myself in the victim's shoes? Or claws? And worry myself sick? Then I found that an owl is unable to fend for himself or catch his own food until at least three months old and Pip was only just over two months of age. That did not help!

35

The fourth day dawned, with a very distressing sight of Pip still frozen to the same spot and still being mobbed by dozens of birds. Something really must be done now! Going to my friend with the telephone I asked if I could please pursue the matter and thankfully she was happy for me to do so, being almost as worried as yours truly about Pip. Ringing Bob the RSPCA inspector again, I asked if he could please, please, please help. This time he said he would see what he could do. He rang back in about an hour and said HELP IS ON THE WAY! Hurrah!

An hour or so later the inspector arrived in his official van shortly followed by the fire engine and a police car with two policemen. They then closed the road off whilst the fire engine made a precarious turn into the driveway of the garden where Pip was being terrorised in the tall tree. Firemen put the extending ladder up the tree and one began to climb slowly up towards Pip, whilst the now gathered crowd of people watched in silence, eyes glued to the brave fireman.

Then, Pip flew off! I could have shot him on the spot! Everyone looked at me, and with a scarlet face I muttered my apologies to the fire crew, the police and the RSPCA Inspector, saying I would send them all a donation as soon as I could, wondering how on earth I could as I was, as always, quite broke. The crowd broke up and everyone went their own way.

I felt just about as foolish as when some years before, when tight skirts became the rage, I wore mine for the first time to go to work one morning on our usual bus. Most of us regular travellers knew each other by then of course. When the bus stopped at North Road station I got off nonchalantly, feeling quite smart in the new fashion. Jumping off the bus as usual my legs were suddenly brought back together again by the restriction of the tightness of the skirt and my feet hit the pavement at a run, running with tiny steps straight for the concrete litter bin at the bus stop. Unable to stop I hit the litter bin, ending up head first in all the rubbish it held, with my legs in the air to the cheering and clapping of the bus-load of fellow travellers! They say, pride comes before a fall, and indeed it does! But I digress, back to Pip.

Where on earth had he gone now and what would happen to him? I worried myself sick all night and barely slept a wink, watching and listening from the bedroom window for any movement or any hooting in the night, but nothing seemed to stir or call.

Next morning the front door bell rang - early. A workman was standing there.

"Mrs Preston, can you come with me please to Waterside - there is an owl in a barrel of water - someone is holding it's head up with a stick, but it looks in poor shape."

We hurried down to Waterside and lo and behold there was poor Pip, looking dead, no movement, just floating wings outstretched with his head being gently held up with a long stick. Was I relieved to see him again! The man who brought me down kindly took me home again and I was able to minister to Pip with food and Dr. Bach Rescue Remedy for the awful trauma he'd just gone through - now the fifth day since his 'escape' from the aviary. He was kept indoors for a couple of days before being taken up into the aviary once more; this time until he was ready to look after himself. Bubbles was glad to see him back again as well! And the Services did eventually receive their donation, small though it was, I'm afraid. When Pip went next time he was fully able to care for himself and we watched as he flew off, having made contact with another Tawny Owl who came to visit him some nights whilst still in the aviary.

Bubbles remained with us for several years in good health, though still much an out-door cat and very independent. One day he went to eat his food in the kitchen with the others but just held his head over the dish, trying to eat but unable to do so. Looking into his mouth I found his teeth very decayed and his gums in a bad way with pyorrhoea, none of which I had noticed before as he never seemed in trouble. Taking him to the vet right away, we found when the good vet checked his chest the poor lad also had pneumonia. Bubbles' back teeth were removed under anaesthetic and he was given antibiotics before being brought home again.

But next day Bubbles was unable to walk and became increasingly paralysed. I was unsure what to do for the best for him, and held him on his back, on my lap, as he had some drops of Rescue Remedy and Crab apple as the cleanser and purifier. Speaking to him whilst looking into his eyes I asked him how he felt and wished he could talk to me to let me know what he would like. On saying that to him he winked his right eye. I asked if he was indicating something with his right eye winking, and he again winked it. Was he indicating a 'yes'? If so, would he indicate a 'no' answer - his left eye winked.

For the next three days Bubbles and I communicated in this way through his eyes by my questions. He was getting daily weaker and taking only liquid food and drops of water. Bubbles said he knew he was going to die, but that he must see the vet again. Asking him if the vet was going to help him he 'said' the vet had the healing gift and he needed to be with him for a short while. I suggested he would like to stay there the night but he winked furiously with his left eye - NO! NO! He said he was not afraid of dying. I wanted him to tell me that he could be healed but he replied that he could not be.

Bubbles 'told' me he would die early on Saturday morning but that he would return to tell me he was alright - and I wondered how he would return. Sitting up with him cradled in my arms all Friday night I was anxious about his laboured breathing. He told me his time to leave was eight o'clock and as we neared that time, with tears in my eyes I asked "Are you nearly ready to go now, Bubbles?" His eyes looked into mine then both gently closed - he was very, very tired.

At eight o'clock on that Saturday morning, I asked him "But you will come back and tell me you are alright?" He winked another "Yes" with his right eye, breathed a deep final breath and was gone. My tears scattered over his still, warm body. I laid it out, putting a candle by his head and some flowers from the garden by his tabby body, now at total peace.

That night I went to bed, desolate, and dropped into sleep eventually. Then found myself walking through the back garden in sleep state - which is a wonderful state of Reality. On the little flat wall at the top of the garden - there was Bubbles! More clear and alive than when in the physical body,

I smiled at him and asked if that was the way he'd 'come back' to let me know he was alright. He gave a broad grin which lifted his whiskers and as I wondered how he was now feeling he gave a very marked "YES" of feeling fine, with his right eye.

When Dennis and I buried his physical body under a rose bush in the front garden, it was with the knowing that it was only his body we were burying now - not Bubbles himself - he was fine, well and happy, I knew, for sure.

He was safely at Home, where I have asked all my loved ones to wait for me, and not to reincarnate, as they often do, of course, like humans who need or want to. Yes I have very fond memories of The Owl and the Pussycat!

Jackie the Jackdaw

Jackie the Jackdaw was brought in as a baby, beak wide open for food and starving. How long she had been without her parents was anyone's guess as none were seen around the area where she was found. It is always best to leave young birds where they are, if no cats or predators are ready to pounce, as their parents will usually find them or know where they are to continue feeding. I always feel nature has gone wrong in that young birds, unable to fly properly or find their own food, leave their nest and are at the mercy of everything for several days (or weeks maybe, in some cases) until they can take off and fend for themselves.

So, Jackie, the Jackdaw, became a further member of the family. As she became older, her night time perch was on a swivel rail conveniently over the old kitchen sink, where droppings could be washed down easily. Breakfast was a battle. Her favourite breakfast was my cornflakes! If she could get her feet as well as her beak in the bowl, I'd had it! She ate just about everything we did - AND at the same time if she could. Having the freedom of the house, if any small object went missing, I eventually realised where to look for it first - behind any of the pictures hanging on the walls. Pulling out the bottom of the picture all sorts of things would tumble out - cotton reels, sweets, small scissors, paper clips, pencils, bits of paper, nail files - she 'collected' everything she could lay her beak on. A favourite game was to pick up clothes pegs and lose them for me. So I would put one on her beak - and she'd be furious! I thought it taught her a lesson…

Then came the day when it was time to let her fly free and make her own life out there in the big world. Jackie took off out the open kitchen window in great delight. Freedom! And look! Clothes pegs! On washing lines! All over the place! With great gusto she began pulling out each and every peg she could see. Neighbours' washing went flying everywhere in the wind. Oh Lord, I had never thought of that consequence! Thankfully, after the initial spree, Jackie left clothes pegs alone, she had got her own back on them and that was that!

One evening she had not returned home again, in the kitchen window, and I was very worried. The front door bell rang and I went through to the hall to answer it. Two Boy Scouts were standing on the doorstep holding a carrier bag. "Is this yours?" one asked, opening out the bag. Looking into, it I found one sorry looking jackdaw. It was Jackie. She had over-stepped the mark, flown up into the recreational field where a lot of people were waiting for the official Fire Work Display to start, on the 5th November and not content with just watching what was going on, she decided to help out a bit and began picking up various fireworks from the big container and flying off with them, dropping them into the tops of trees and other places - no doubt down chimney pots, as well. She could not pick up the larger fireworks, but did very well in carting off the smaller ones, until she was caught and carted off home again. Thankfully, folk took it in good humour and she was not hung, drawn and quartered on the spot.

Another evening she arrived back in a carrier bag, a different one this time. She had flown into the fish and chip shop at the bottom of the main street, and perched precariously on the handle of the lid of one of the huge chip fryers, with gallons of fat bubbling just underneath her. A brave assistant threw a tea towel over her and to the cheers of the shop full of people, put the captive in a carrier bag, knowing just where to bring her.

But Jackie did not meet with cheers when she decided to see what a local ladies hairdressers salon was like! She apparently walked in the open door and there, before her, was an Aladdin's Cave! Curlers, hairgrips, hairnets, bits of this and bits of that - wonderful! Sorting out all these treasures was going to be great fun! But the shrieks and screams of the ladies under the dryers and having their hair-do's were most upsetting for her as she flew around getting more and more panic-stricken. A towel was thrown over her and she was subdued and brought home in disgrace.

Getting ready for work one lunchtime (I was part-time then with British Rail). Jackie was sitting on her perch over the kitchen sink. The window was open and I was waiting for her to fly out for the afternoon, as I was cleaning my two false

41

teeth in front of it. Suddenly she swooped down on my shoulder and had a little poke around in my ear, one of her many pleasures with people, before flying straight out of the window, which I was then about to close. Looking at my hand to rinse off my teeth before putting them back in, I saw to my horror that they had disappeared. On no!!! "Jackie, where are my teeth?"

Racing outside to the courtyard, I looked up and there she was, proudly standing on the corner of the rooftop, holding my teeth and wondering where the best hiding place would be

Clapping my hands loudly I shouted through the gap in my mouth "Jackie, give me back my teeth!" AND SHE DID! She dropped them straight down into my waiting hands.

Thankfully I caught them, and did not have to face an office full of chaps chanting "All I want for Christmas is my two front teeth." That was what I got when the dentist took them out in the first place years before, owing to his bungled work.

Another day Jackie went AWOL and as I was scanning the view from the upstairs front window, I noticed a movement in our neighbour's window. On no!! She was holding something in her beak and trying to get out of the window with it. Shamefacedly I went downstairs, knocked on the next-door and asked if I could please have my jackdaw back. Then our neighbour who was terrified of birds (many people are I find, unfortunately) went upstairs and screamed! I raced up - and found Jackie had created havoc in her bedroom - she had obviously walked in the open front door (it was safe to leave one's door open in those days...), gone up into the front bedroom and had a wonderful time for ages, pulling things around and hiding things.

But that was it as far as our neighbour was concerned. Jackie had to be put down or kept locked up for life in one of our aviaries. I spent the rest of the afternoon in tears and worry, not being able to do either with our friend the jackdaw. She really had blotted her copybook this time.

Desperate to know what to do, Jackie had to be confined to the aviary, which she hated, 'jacking' away constantly to be let out and fly her freedom. Eventually an idea occurred. Would Mr.H.G.Hurrell, the well-known naturalist, be willing to accept her at his home and grounds at South Brent in Devon? Yes, he would be happy to have her, he replied, if we took her up. Dennis and I drove her to Mr.Hurrell's home, set on the edge of the moor, at Moorgate as it was called. He took her into a large aviary, and I carried in her favourite foods and left a supply with him, of course. She followed us frantically around the aviary, jacking all the while and my heart was breaking to have to leave her there, feeling a traitor to a lovely friend who trusted me.

Mr. Hurrell showed us the pine martens he had - fascinating creatures, and other animals and birds - including Atlanta, the seal, who had her own large pool. We found it amazing when, swimming underwater, he would call out "Atlanta - number four please" and she would surface, flap onto the surrounding path of the pool, and point with a flipper at the four number in a row of one to ten. She did this, with different numbers, time and again, all correctly. Could she hear underwater - or was she telepathic?

We went up several week-ends with stocks of her favourite goodies, until one day we had a letter to say she had escaped the aviary and had joined a local group of jackdaws, so it was a terrific relief that she was at last free again and to join her own kind. I tried never to make such a friend of a wild bird again as it obviously brings them great problems when it comes to release. But invariably it happens that one gets very attached to the little patient, bird or animal and it often ends in heartache, unfortunately, as the majority of folk do not share the same feelings or understandings, of course. However, I trust that Jackie will be among one of the first to greet me when it is my time to leave my physical body for the next dimension - I hope there will be hundreds of 'first to say hello' again! It is good to know our animal and bird friends live on, as well as our loved human friends, and that the link of love never dies.

Ginger

The neighbours' children came to our door one day to say there was a terribly poorly ginger cat in our garden with parts of each leg rotten to the bone. Eventually I was able to catch him but he was very wild, angry and terrified. Getting him into a large cat basket was a feat of courage and strength in itself. I then prepared a large caged area at the top of the garden and put food, water and a litter tray in for him. Part filling the bath upstairs with warm, slightly salted water, I took the basket up, put on thick gardening gloves and managed to get the snarling creature by the scruff of the neck, lowering him into the water. Flicking off a glove, I splashed the water over his poor legs, washing the terrible sores as well as possible.

Suddenly, the back door bell rang, all three dogs barked their heads off and the cat tore out of the bath and up the bathroom curtains at a rate of knots.

I saw to the visitor and later cautiously opened the bathroom door. The cat was demented and it took all my courage to catch him again and get him back in the basket with its towel lining. An hour or two later when he had dried off in the warm bathroom, I took him in the basket up to the top of the garden and let him out in the large caged area. He went straight for the dish of food and I backed out very quickly. On his food and into his drink I had put the wonderful Dr.Edward Bach Flower Remedies of Rescue Remedy for the shock he had been put through, Crab Apple as the cleanser and purifier, Holly for his anger and hatred and Walnut for the great change in his life.

When I came down into the house again I wondered where all the blood was coming from - it was my right arm! When the cat had raced out of the bath earlier, after the bell went and the dogs barked, he had obviously scratched my arm quite badly, but I had pulled my sleeves down and not noticed until the blood soaked through the sleeve of my blouse and jumper. It looked very messy, but I cleaned it up and got on with things.

That night my hand and arm began to ache dreadfully and swell up - a red line went ominously up the whole arm. Next morning, after a painful and sleepless night I saw to the cat, and all the other animals and birds, and went to a neighbour who could heal and asked him for healing help. He took one look at it and said he would not touch it - I had to go to hospital and get it seen to properly. In those days I had a lot more courage than today, and went to another friend to ask for her healing help. Edna looked at my arm and told me to go straight to the hospital, just down the road from us here. "No Edna, I would like you to give me healing, please." She finally agreed and asked for healing, during which I closed my eyes, sitting on her chair, with her hands over my head, and then I 'saw' the cat, in such a dreadful condition, in my arms lying quite contentedly there, his four legs were in a far worse state than my one arm and hand - how must he be feeling?? Tears started to pour down my face, as I really felt for him; pity and compassion poured into the cat and a great peace came to me. In a voice not her own, Edna said, "My child, hatred cannot live where love abides." The pain had died down and the inflammation and I was able to walk home, knowing that all would be well.

Next morning my hand and arm were almost back to normal and cleared up very quickly after that, and I was most grateful to Edna and Whoever did this miraculous healing through her.

Ginger's legs also began to heal rapidly after that, but even so, each day I took my life in my hands by going into his cage and putting fresh food and water down, and whilst he was so engaged on that, cleaning out his litter tray, which he obligingly used.

Came the day to get him doctored. A friend with a car very kindly came and helped greatly with that, and brought him back again. Then came the great query - what to do with him? Who'd have such an aggressive cat? He had calmed down a lot, but I still had to wear Wellington boots and thick gloves to go into his cage and couldn't keep him in there forever.

One night, keeping our dog/cat flap closed and locked, much to our three dogs and five cats' annoyance, I took up Ginger's food and water, with my wellies and gloves safely on, put it down for him and slipped out of the pen, leaving the door slightly open, with a brick to keep it so. I scuttled down the path as quick as possible and breathed a sigh of relief when in the house. It was about midnight and all ours had been out and were safely gathered in and the wild birds and animals were safe in their enclosures. Hopefully, Ginger would find his way back to his freedom and roaming again.

During the night, the screams of catfights rent the air and my heart sank. Ginger! Next morning, on opening the door to let our cats and dogs out, my heart sank again to find Ginger on the doorstep! Oh no! He had decided to stay then! Hurriedly shutting the door before our crowd went out and were attacked, I donned my Wellingtons - you will be wondering why, so I will explain that if Ginger saw legs in front or around him he would race for them, wrapping his forelegs around them, digging in with his claws in full fury - it was a dickens of a job to get him off, so I took all necessary precautions, of course. After getting a dish piled with food, I put on heavy gloves, put our cats and dogs in another part of the house, closing that door, and opened the back door - with Ginger sitting patiently on the doorstep still. Holding the dish way out in front of me, Ginger glued his eyes on it and we travelled up the garden path together. Going into the pen, I put the dish on the floor and he was on it like a flash. I crept out and shut the door behind me very quickly! At least he was safely out of trouble for the day. I didn't let him out that night. Two or three nights later I tried again - and screams of cats tore through the night air. I couldn't inflict this on them - yet equally I couldn't keep Ginger penned up.

A friend came to visit one day and we caught up on a lot of things and I told her about the ginger cat in the pen in the garden - she decided she did not want to meet him, thanks, even though she liked cats and had one of her own which was also ginger.

On leaving via the front door, she was halfway down the path when suddenly, over the garden wall sprang a large ginger cat. "That's Ginger!" I shouted. "Stay still, whatever you do!" Ginger was just a few feet away from her and eyeing her legs with a wicked gleam in his eyes. How on earth he had got out of his locked pen we had no idea but out he was and a danger to anyone in his path.

"Marilyn - HELP!"

"Stay there, I'll get a plate of food for him and lead him up into his pen. Don't move!"

"Marilyn - I'm spending a penny….."

With that I watched as a little stream trickled down the path and our friend was frozen to the spot.

I ran in, quickly got a plate of food and raced out again, but not before pulling on the wellies and grabbing a thick pair of gloves. Calling Ginger and holding the plate in front of me, with his eyes glued, as before, to the dish which he readily recognised, we went over the little wall, up the garden path and safely into his cage again. Making sure the door was locked (why wasn't it before, I asked myself?) I hurried back to my friend who came back into the house to clean up and have a cup of tea with Rescue Remedy, before making her way home again. Not surprisingly we didn't see her again for quite some time after that.

We look back on the event with laughter now, but it was anything but funny at the time.

The friend who took Ginger to the vet for me to get him doctored came again one day and asked what was going to happen to him. I was at my wits end and told her so. "Leave it to me for a few days and I will see what I can do", she said. She had been a marvellous animal welfare worker whilst in Singapore with her husband in the Forces, and saw some appalling cruelty to animals there, helping wherever she could and catching many ill, sick and wounded cats and dogs, who had been left to fend for themselves when Forces families moved on, leaving their 'pets' behind.

A few days later, Julie came back with the astounding news that she thought she had found a good home for Ginger.

"With people?" I asked incredulously.

"Yes - with people - kind people!"

"Have you told them how dangerous he is?"

"Well….Yes"

I knew these good people, they had taken on a cat who had been very ill when brought here a few years before and it had a wonderful home with them until it 'died' several years later. And now they were willing to take on this one! I explained to Julie that I could not let them take on Ginger without telling them the whole truth about him.

"I'm sure they realise what the position is" Julie said and with that out came her large cat basket, on went a pair of stout gloves and in she went, fearlessly, into Ginger's pen. Off they both went in her car and I was left wondering how on earth it was all going to work out.

But amazingly, work out it did! After a few days of getting used to each other, Ginger got his feet under the table well and truly and took up his night-time place - lying between the couple in bed! Mind you, they were very careful when they moved in the night to turn over - Ginger would put in his grumbles in no uncertain terms, but it was quite miraculous that he had found such a wonderful and kind home.

Some years later, the kindly couple were deeply upset when Ginger developed cancer of the mouth, and though they had all the treatment the vet could give, as well as healing here, Ginger had to be 'put to sleep'. They missed him deeply and proudly brought me a lovely photograph of him in their doorway, when he was in his prime, enjoying the sunshine and I'm sure, keeping any intruders out.

The National Federation of Spiritual Healers

I came across the National Federation of Spiritual Healers, when attending a healing demonstration given by the world famous healer, Harry Edwards, of Shere, near Guildford. It was amazing watching him work, in a matter of minutes he could achieve miracles. I have never been able to achieve such quick results, well, not very often! He asked me if I would like to become a member of the N.F.S.H and this would mean submitting several references written by people as testimonials of their betterment or cure, or for their pets.

In October, in 1971, I therefore submitted to Mr.Edwards, as President, and his team of Vice-President, Chairman, Treasurer and Administrator, seven animal healing testimonials written by owners, and eight healing testimonies of humans, and was immediately accepted as a full healer member.

I only wish there were photocopiers in those days, to have kept copies, but I copied the letters and have kept these, from which I now quote below, to give you some idea of what healing can do for animals. As this book is only concerned with healing animals, the human stories are not quoted. These were only a fraction of the cases dealt with, of course, and used only for verification to become an N.S.F.H member at the time.

Extracts from animal healing testimonials:-

"In the month of March 1971, my father-in-law's 14 year old dog, Bobbie, was taken ill with a stroke. The power in his back legs was gone. After examination, the vet said the dog was too far gone and the best thing for it was to be put down. We heard of Mrs.M.Preston of Saltash, in Cornwall, and we took the dog to her. After four visits and the dog being on her absent healing list, the dog is now running around, and also getting up and down steps…we are very grateful"

NGE - Devon

"In February of this year my cat had a fall in my kitchen, as a result, losing the use of his back legs and tail. I went to the vets who gave treatment for a week. Although the use came back to the tail and back legs, the paws would not lay flat and there was no use in the paws either - this made it very painful and difficult to walk. My cat's name is 'Puggy'. The tops of his paws, which he was walking on (being bent underneath), were raw and bleeding all the time. A couple of months later I heard of and went to see Mrs.Marilyn Preston...After the first visit, the very next day one of the paws was out straight; the next week I returned and a few days later the other paw was out flat. My cat now runs, jumps and is back to normal...."

LM- Devon

"My dog had suffered from an allergy for several months when I first heard of Mrs.M.Preston. I wrote to her and she came to see me. He had been seen by a vet and although he didn't get any worse, he didn't get any better. When Mrs. Preston saw him she put her hands on the dog and after a few minutes he became cool for a week and did not scratch at all. Mrs.Preston came several times and each time a great improvement was noticed. The dog is now well and I am thankful...."

GMS - Cornwall

"When this world is fit for animals to live in we can consider ourselves civilised. At the moment lethargy stands in the way of civilisation. We are a nation of pet, not animal, lovers, and Mrs.Preston shows us the difference. Three veterinary surgeons told us that our little dog's nose complaint could not be cured. Mrs.Preston is curing him rapidly, and we shall always be grateful....It proves that the cruelty of vivisection is not necessary. We wallow along in the abomination of the Dark Ages, because we are too lazy to explore the method which was shown to us 2,000 years ago by Christ".

AS - Surrey

"This is to recount my own personal experience of Spiritual Healing with Mrs.Marilyn Preston of Saltash. Earlier this year I took one of the children's pet cockerels to her, suffering from a deformed foot. The bird had been walking on a stump as the toes of the foot had turned inwards, and indeed the toes seemed to be withering away. The cockerel had been like this some two months or more, and the verdict of knowledgeable poultry keepers around, was that it should be 'put down' as it could only hobble and was being constantly tormented by the other birds in the flock. "

"Mrs.Preston kept it some ten days at her home. When I called to collect the bird, the foot was no longer turned under but was, to all intents and purposes, a normal cockerel's foot with claws stretching to the front. The bird itself was in good spirits. Since then, although we expected the foot to revert to it's previous position, this has not occurred, and the bird today walks normally and perches, and is, in fact, very able to take care of himself! Looking at him now I do not think anyone would know that he had once suffered a deformity. He has needed no further treatment since Mrs.Preston had him. I am open-minded as to the significance of Spiritual Healing, but am certain in this particular instance that Mrs.Preston was able to affect a miraculous cure. I would not hesitate to take any sick animal to her in the future".

PABBC - Cornwall

"On Sunday 1st August 1971, my dog, Candy was very ill indeed and had been so for a week previously. The following day I took her to the vet, who said she had congestion of the lungs and was in a critical condition - I was told to take her again on the Friday...As there was no improvement by the Thursday, I was very worried and took her to see Mrs.Preston of Saltash who gave my dog healing and said she was suffering from St.Vitus Dance through Distemper and Hardpad. On the Friday I returned to the vets. He then said that my dog was suffering from St.Vitus Dance through Distemper and Hardpad and that she would have the

St.Vitus Dance for the rest of her life. On the Monday another vet saw my dog and told me the St.Vitus Dance was very bad and that she was in a very bad way altogether. I was asked to call again if she was no better by the Friday.

At this time we thought the dog was going to die and in fact the neighbours said it was a shame we did not have her put down, for she screamed with pain when touched and spent the time with her nose on the ground and going into dark corners. A third vet's opinion was wanted by my vets. This vet confirmed Candy had St.Vitus Dance, Distemper and Hardpad, and also a large abscess in the ear. Her temperature was 104 degrees. My dog is only two years old and had been fully vaccinated against Distemper and Hardpad, with the course of Epivax. On the Friday, Candy's temperature was still 104 degrees and the abscess terrible. The vet advised me to have a lot of old cloths handy for when the abscess burst. I went to see Mrs.Preston again on the Saturday, and she gave further contact healing.

The following morning, when I went to see Candy, everything was gone! There was no swelling whatsoever, and there was no twitch from the St.Vitus Dance! I rang the vet and said that it was a miracle...he replied "The last five tablets have done it!"

But I know differently and am convinced that Spiritual Healing has cured my pet when she was a dying dog"

M.A.P.T, Cornwall

I cannot take credit for any of the hundreds of healings, which have taken place here over the years, either with contact or absent healing, with animals or humans, as I honestly don't know how they are achieved. I only know there is a Higher Power which can be called on to help and have often been greatly privileged in watching as miracles happened, but again not always. It is always a great disappointment when nothing seems to help and vets and doctors have done their utmost too. It's strange that when healings take place I don't personally feel responsible, yet if nothing seems to happen to help, then I do!

Mrs G and her Budgerigar

One morning a lady came to our front door asking for help for her budgie. Would I go to see it, please, as she was sure the vet would have to put it down. But first, she was visiting her very sick husband in hospital, just along the road from us here, and would call in again in about an hour on her way home, to take me there to see to her budgie. She explained that the bird had his "wing up around his back". Questioning her I asked what on earth she meant, to which she replied she could not understand it herself, but his leg was just "sticking up in the air behind his back".

I came back into our house wondering deeply about this strange phenomenon, and said aloud "Will you get that poor budgie's leg down please?" and got on with all the jobs, which needed to be done.

An hour was up and another ring at the front doorbell. I went with the lady to her home, walking through the park. Noticing she was holding her arm rather awkwardly, I asked if it was all right. She replied that she had injured it and had seen a specialist, but now it was worse, after treatment; being extremely painful; she also said she had very painful ears and one was discharging badly. I asked her name and then Mrs G broke down, saying she was unable to take any more pain and worry and had decided to take her own life at the weekend, as it was not worth living.

On reaching her home, Mrs G showed me the budgie in his cage and was amazed to see his leg was now down, but hanging limply. She tried to explain how it had been sticking up in the air for three days, making walking or climbing almost impossible and being unable to get to his food or drink. I asked her if I could bring the budgie home with me to care for and tend to his leg. She agreed to this willingly.

I asked the lady if she would like to try some healing as it might help her painful arm, but I could not promise it would put it right. She said if I thought it would do any good, she'd "have a go" but did not believe in it and had no faith. I explained she did not have to believe in healing, nor did she have to have any faith, just a willingness to try it, if she'd like to.

Holding her right wrist, where the damage had occurred, she said "Oh! Aren't your hands lovely and cold! I am always too hot and would love to feel cold like your hands." Coldness being the bane of my life, I said she really would not like to feel like this at all - it is miserable - especially in the winter when I cannot keep warm even with the maximum amount of clothes on, plus the central heating...

We both went quiet and I mentally asked for healing help to come to Mrs G. if this was in order for her to receive it, please. After a few minutes, she started to pull her arm away, but I mentally asked her to relax and allow the healing to take place, and her arm relaxed again. After a while, taking

my hands away from her arm, I asked Mrs G. how she was feeling.

"WELL! What an experience!" she replied. "I could feel my arm going numb, but then it was as though a thousand brass bands were playing in my ears and I tried to take my hand away to put both hands up to my ears as the noise was unbearable. Then I felt I had to relax and the noise died away - as did all the pain in my ears! And there is no pain in my wrist or arm now....." She was amazed and very relieved and I walked home with the budgie and cage. On coming into my home again, I called aloud "Will you take Mrs G's temperature down, please, as she is far too hot all the time."

Putting the budgie and cage down in the breakfast room, where I had four or five more budgies in a huge cage in an alcove, I asked the little chap how on earth he had got his leg up around his back as his owner had said. Whereupon he looked up at me, chirped, and fell off his perch onto the floor of his cage, upside down. He then proceeded to try to right himself, but only succeeded in putting his very short leg through his extremely long primary feathers to awkwardly climb up the side of the cage onto the perch, so that he was now standing on and through his wing. Shortly tiring of this he put his wing back in its rightful position but could no way get his leg untangled from his wing, consequently his leg was then sticking up in the air behind his back! If I had not witnessed it myself, there was no way I could have imagined how this could happen. Gradually, I taught him how to untangle his leg from his wing; so that it was no longer a problem for him and his owner was happy for him to live on here with my own budgies. Not liking birds kept in captivity any more than wild animals in confinement, when they passed over at the end of their earthly lives, I did not keep any more.

But back to Mrs G…Next morning brought her back again, looking very worried indeed, "Mrs Preston, I don't know what is happening to me but last night I was absolutely freezing and even had to have my husband's hot water bottle which I've never had in my life before, and his wool hat and socks on in bed - I thought I was going to die!"
"Oh dear - I asked yesterday for your temperature to be taken down, but it never occurred to me to say "stop when it is comfortable' as I really did not think my request was going to be granted!"

Mrs G. replied "Oh that's alright if it's you doing it." And she went on her way to the hospital again to visit her husband.

Some months later, the lady was calling on me again - her wrist had 'gone out', using the same floor cleaning apparatus which caused it to be damaged before, as she did cleaning work in the area, to make ends meet. I gave her healing and she was much relieved and helped.

But a few months further on, and the same thing happened once more. More healing and thankfully relief again. After she had left I fell to thinking about this recurring problem with her wrist and arm. Her ears were fine and she'd had no further trouble with them, she was glad to report.

Next day was Sunday and my parents were coming over to join Dennis and I for Sunday lunch. So for me it was to be a hectic time cleaning the house, seeing to all the birds and animals and then prepare the meal for the four of us. Cleaning the lounge, I found myself thinking of Mrs G. and her arm again, and sat down on the settee, Vacuum cleaner now silent. Going into a daydream I mentally went out to the kitchen, reached in a cupboard and took out a tin of Plaster of Paris, which is normally used to plaster birds' or small animals' legs, if broken, when they were brought into my small Wild Bird and Animal Hospital here, in those days.

Mentally I searched for some 'mutton cloth' and suddenly remembered I had some new net curtaining in a drawer. All still in my mind, I visualised putting a piece of this net around Mrs G's wrist and arm; dipping the Plaster of Paris roll in a container of warm water, and wrapping this firmly but not too tightly round and round her wrist and arm, turning and smoothing the ends of the net back over at wrist and in front of the elbow so that it was comfortable to wear without rubbing the hand or elbow joint when the 'patient' was using her hand and arm. The plaster appeared to dry instantly and I can still hear the hollow sounding noise it made as I tested it by tapping with my fingertips.

Suddenly opening my eyes, I looked at the clock - eleven o'clock!! I had sat down, just for a quick minute and had just wasted ten precious minutes of hurried cleaning time before having to start preparing lunch! Fool!

Next morning, a ring at the front doorbell found Mrs G. on the doorstep once more. She came into the lounge, saying her husband, who was now home again feeling much better, said she was not to see me any more as he thought she was going 'funny'. Holding out her right arm, she asked me to look at it to see if I could see anything different. Puzzled, I studied it, wondering what to look for - it seemed perfectly normal to me, and this I told her. She then explained that there was Plaster of Paris fixed on her arm, as firm as a rock and she could not understand why her husband and now I could not see it!

Looking with amazement at the woman, I asked what time she felt it go on. She thought for a moment and said it must have been somewhere around quarter to eleven, the day before, as she always listened to a special radio programme at that time on a Sunday. I explained that I had been day-dreaming at that precise time the day before, thinking that I was only thinking about it and never realising for a moment that she would be receiving it, albeit not on a physical level as we could not see it. We had never heard of such a thing happening and did not know it was possible. Mrs G. was tremendously relieved to know it was only me 'doing it' and went off happily again with her 'plastered' and comfortable arm. Three weeks later the plaster 'dissolved' and her arm gave her no more trouble, thankfully.

This happened more than thirty years ago, before we had heard of visualisation or working with the mind to assist with healing, so it was a great and happy surprise to know such things were possible.

Victoria

Some considerable time after the amazing experience with Mrs G, I was taking our three dogs out in the pouring rain in the evening, when a friend came up to us and asked if I had seen a ginger cat anywhere, "with a hind leg dragging behind it?" It had been hit by a car in the afternoon, and she had been unable to trace where it had gone, but thought it had dragged itself into a nearby garden which was heavily overgrown. Looking over the gate of the garden, I called and listened but could hear nothing but the drumming rain on my umbrella, whilst the dogs got soaking wet.

Three days later, a gentleman came to the door and asked if I would pick up a stray cat, which he had just found in his garden, lying under a shrub, badly injured. Going to his home with him, he handed me a forlorn looking ginger cat, with one hind leg hanging straight down.

I brought the cat home and wondered what to do about her whilst I made her as comfortable as possible in our bathroom - the only room in the house where she would be undisturbed by the dogs, cats, rabbit, pigeon and hen who all lived in the house with us, which they much preferred to the garden. Giving her a little food and drink, which she took with great relish, I settled her in a comfortable cat basket with a litter tray close by and closely watched her, mentally asking what best to do.

Then my Inner Voice spoke, asking me to "Remember the fox cub. Take her to the same vet in Devon where you will be told again that nothing can be done to help her. This is a 'test case' for animal healing. You are to bring her home with you and give her healing."

I placed advertisements all around the town and in the press over the following few days but no-one claimed the ginger cat.

But meanwhile I took the cat, who was quite regal despite her shattered hind keg - now sporting the name Victoria which suited her admirably - to the vet in question and asked his opinion. He examined the leg, which was broken in several places and felt like a bag of bones inside the amazingly unbroken skin, shook his head and said he would have to put her down right away as she was beyond operation, especially as she had lain for three days in terrible weather and was obviously suffering from shock, and she would certainly never use the leg again. I did not mention that Victoria had been having Dr.Bach's Remedy since the day before when she came under my care, which is marvellous for shocks and accidents, of course, for humans, animals, birds and plants.

Victoria looked at me and continued to purr. The vet said it was quite unusual to have an all-ginger female cat - they usually had some white on them somewhere, but Vicky had none. I explained that I was taking her home again and would give her healing. To his great credit, the vet was furious, saying that it was cruel to keep the cat alive in that terrible condition and that nothing could heal the shattered leg. He asked for my name and address and said he would take the matter further. I realised that as far as he was concerned, and with all his medical expertise and experience, there probably was nothing that could be done by orthodox methods - I was grateful that he cared so much for an animal and did not want it to suffer further - but having seen so many miracles occur here and with absent healing, I followed the instructions of Inner Voice which I used to hear at times in those days.

For the following ten days, Victoria settled happily into her home in the bathroom, and each day I gave her healing and the Dr.Bach Remedies. But nothing happened to her leg! It remained totally a 'bag of bones' and dragged after her when she moved anywhere in the room, but she continued to purr loudly whenever we were together and I felt she was not suffering in any way at all.

I began to feel sick with worry - surely The Voice was not wrong?? It had stated categorically that this was to be a 'test case' for animal healing - but no healing was taking place. What on earth was I to do now, Lord?

Giving her her supper she settled down to sleep and I washed and got ready for bed - it was near midnight and I had to be up early in the morning, as usual. All the other birds and animals had been fed, the dogs exercised, and jobs finished for the night and Dennis had already gone to bed.

Then I found myself going downstairs again and going into the lounge, where I sat down. In despair, on the settee, wondering what to do and asking God for help for Victoria. It came into my mind about Mrs G's 'mental operation' and I went deep into thought.....

Closing my eyes, suddenly there was what I knew to be a very rare and precious vase before me. But it was shattered in small pieces and it was my task to mend it, without a crack showing when it was together again. I mentally pictured a tube of 'invisible glue' and began the job of putting the jigsaw of the vase together again, sticking each piece with the tube of glue until the vase was whole and beautiful once more. I admired the handiwork...Then the Voice said my job was now to do this to Victoria's broken leg!

I envisaged a tube of 'Bone Glue' and set about the new task of finding and fitting together in their right place, all Vicky's small pieces of bone, glueing each piece in place with the special, brilliant Bone Glue. When all were neatly and beautifully in place, I mentally wrapped the structure in a sort of 'living Sellotape' so it was held quite firmly in place. Next the muscles, ligaments, blood vessels, flesh and tissue needed to be put back in their correct positions, and though I know nothing about such a procedure, I did what I thought appropriate and visualised it as being perfect again.

The 'daydreaming' or rather 'midnight-dreaming' came to an abrupt end when The Voice said "It is done!" and I went back up to bed feeling relaxed and comfortable and wondering what is was all about.

The next morning, I got up and went into the bathroom to wash and dress - Victoria shot out of the door and raced down the stairs, on all four normal legs! Perhaps I should have been amazed, but it all seemed perfectly natural and I shouted out "How did You do that, then? Thank You!" Following her, I felt Victoria's hind leg which was perfectly healed - there was no difference between either back leg and she simply joined the other cats for breakfast as though she had been here all her life!

That morning John, a reporter from the Sunday Express came for healing again and asked me if anything interesting had been happening. I pointed to Victoria, who was lying along the top of an armchair in the lounge, and told him about the events, though not mentioning about the 'mental operation' of the night before.

John was totally intrigued as I told him, whilst at the same time channelling healing to his nose which had been broken yet again from another rugby game. He asked if he could have the story for the Sunday Express, explaining that there would be no fee for it. I replied I would love him to tell the story, in order to give readers the opportunity of knowing that even though nothing perhaps could be done medically for a loved one or for themselves or their pets, maybe healing could help, though no promises could be made, of course. Some seem to be able to receive miracles more so than others, it appears.

John asked if he could telephone the Devon vet to get his story and went down to the town to ring him, as we had no phone here in those days. He came back saying he had telephoned and asked the vet if he remembered a lady from Saltash bringing in an all ginger female cat with a shattered hind leg some eleven days before, which he had advised to be put down immediately because of the severity of the condition. The vet thought the reporter was writing an article to publicise my cruelty and told him that he had stated to me at the time that "There is absolutely nothing that can heal this shattered leg. It is absolutely cruel to keep her alive in this condition."

Then John dropped the bombshell that the cat was perfectly healed, that he had seen and felt the leg and there was nothing wrong with it now. The vet said he could not accept the cat was alright and that he would have to examine it himself- I was to take Victoria in as soon as possible.

I then went down to the town to telephone and make an appointment for the following day's visit to the vet with Victoria. The veterinary surgeon spoke to me, when the receptionist told him I was on the line. He was quite angry and said he could not possibly accept such a story, without examining the cat himself. We made the appointment and just as I was putting the telephone down, it came to me to ask "I will be able to stay with you while you examine the cat?"

"No, I am sorry I cannot allow that"

"Well, can John, the reporter, stay with you during the examination please?"

"No, he certainly can't!" came the reply.

"In that case," said I "there is no way I am bringing her in for any examination. What are you going to do with her that we may not see?" The vet replied that it was none of my business!

John and I had a nice cup of coffee together and he went off with his story for the following Sunday's paper.

And he did a marvellous job! The headlines ran something like "Housewife's Hands Cures Miracle Cat", and told the story as it was - without the part of the visualisation of course, as I thought that would be stretching even John's imagination too far.

The vet then contacted me saying that he would take me to the High Court as it was making the veterinary profession out to be fools. My reply was that that was the last thing I would ever want to do, I had the greatest respect for the wonderful work the veterinary profession does - I would not like the job for anything, and think they are quite marvellous. What I wanted people to realise was that there is a Power which is greater than known on the earth at present and that they can sometimes tap into that great Power to enable it to work It's wonders to help them.

I was very gratified to then learn that the Editor of the Sunday Express said that the paper would take on any legal fees if such a case actually arose. As I was telling the truth and nothing but the truth I was not afraid of any repercussions. Fortunately, the matter went no further, so it did not arise. I was sorry, though that the vet took it personally like that as it was never intended to be anything personal whatsoever. Just that God sometimes takes over and can do things that we mortals can usually only dream about.

Croakey the Crow

A young crow was brought in for help from Torpoint in Cornwall. It was in a most terrible condition, unable to walk or fly. Both legs were crippled, bowed as with severe rickets, both feet clenched tightly together and its feathering was the worst I had ever seen in a bird, just spikey apologies for feathers. Its tongue permanently hung out of its mouth so it could not feed itself and it was utterly terrified. No-one knew how it came to be in that pitiful condition.

For a month I tried everything possible to help the unfortunate creature, but nothing proved of any benefit whatsoever for the little chap. Each day I bandaged anew his deformed bowed legs and feet, keeping the toes outstretched

 with taping to pipe cleaners bent to the shape of a natural foot, and hand fed him as he was unable to feed himself or even take a drink on his own. Dozens of other birds and animals were in the process of being cared for - some healed and were freed again, some homed here for the rest of their natural life on this plane; some passed from their physical bodies for new realms.

One Sunday morning I was treating Croakey in the old greenhouse when a friend (who has since emigrated to Canada with her family) popped in to see me. Jennifer looked aghast at the bird. She had received healing herself here and one of her dogs had been healed of an 'incurable' bone condition here, she had seen so many things happen in our home that she was no longer surprised at anything on this subject.

I explained to Jennifer that having tried everything for Croakey (the only sound he could make was a little croak…), I was giving him just one more full week and if there was still no improvement, would telephone the kindly folk at Torpoint who had brought him for help, putting the position to them that there was really no option but to put the bird out of his physical and mental suffering. It was always the last thing I ever wanted to do, and naturally dreaded it, if there was no chance of recovery or betterment.

The following Monday morning I was feeding and treating Croakey again, when I came to the sad conclusion that he was not going to get any better here. Telephoning the Torpoint couple, I explained the situation to them and they were in full agreement Croakey should be put out of his misery. Praying about and for him, and with tears streaming down my face and with breaking heart, I asked his forgiveness for being unable to help or assist him.

As I gently 'put him to sleep', I asked that Croakey please now be happy, free, able to walk and fly perfectly, as he had never been able to do in this lifetime. Facing the blank stone wall of the greenhouse, broken-hearted (some creatures 'get you' like this for some reason) and in deep sadness, I felt I was talking to nothingness and that my thoughts were going nowhere. With a very heavy heart, I put the little, black, twisted body down on its bed, looking at peace, at last. My tears continued to flow and the ache in my heart grew.

On Monday evenings, at that time, several of us used to gather here for our 'Spiritual Evening', talking about various matters of the spirit and seeking answers, sharing ideas, thoughts and events, meditating and asking for healing help for the many people and animals we knew of, who so needed help. This is done in many homes, everywhere, of course. They were happy evenings and we all had much to talk about, share and pray about (I class prayer as 'thinking to Upstairs'; meditation as 'listening to Upstairs'.)

That Monday evening friends were arriving and Jennifer came in also, as she was sometimes able to join us. Coming into the hallway, Jennifer said "What time did you put Croakey down this morning Marilyn?"

"How did you know that, Jenny? I was going to give him another week as I told you yesterday. It was just on ten o'clock actually, and it broke me up…"

With her face one beaming smile, Jennifer replied: "Because at ten this morning, I was in our kitchen and saw something moving over my head. I looked up - and there was Croakey! I have never seen a bird laughing before, but he had a huge grin from ear to ear- his feathers were absolutely marvellous as he flew upwards - and his legs and feet were perfect as well!"

To say that I was delighted was the understatement of the year! A tremendous feeling of thankfulness and happiness welled up in me and I was able to thank, most gratefully and humbly, Whoever had brought this wonderful miracle about. The four things asked for Croakey had been granted him as he passed from his physical body into his new life - to be happy, to be free - to fly and walk perfectly well. What a wonderful answer and gift! And how wonderful it had been shown to Jennifer and not to me, as I or anyone else could have thought it was my own imagination for something that I wanted to happen, and could have simply 'imagined it all'.

It is food for thought that when a loved one leaves the earthly body, we, in our turn, can possibly help greatly, asking that they continue their journey Home in love, peace, happiness and perfection, until we meet there again.

As a famous doctor commented late that very night on television, "There are other Dimensions of Reality!" It's great to see them sometimes!

BBC TV 'Nationwide'

After several radio and television interviews and programmes, as well as coverage in local and national press, the healing work I was doing here in my small Spiritual Healing Hospital for Wild Birds and Animals became more well known. As it was the first and possibly the only one of its kind in this country, at the time, the BBC asked if they could send their 'Nationwide' team to film it.

Bill Jones, the Director arrived with his team and Luke Casey, the presenter, on the 3rd March 1976 and I found the experience thoroughly enjoyable. That morning I'd had terrible doubts as to whether I should go ahead with it or not, knowing that the media can so easily distort, creating a biased, negative viewpoint. As this also involved the work of Dr Edward Bach and his famous Flower remedies, now internationally known and used, I felt that his life's work could be shot to pieces in a few minutes if the programme was slanted against this sort of unorthodox treatment.

The director and team could not have been nicer, and later, whilst awaiting transmission of the programme with some trepidation, I received a lovely letter from him ending with "The film has been scheduled to run on a number of occasions and has always been squeezed out at the last moment by more 'newsy' events. Have no fear it will be transmitted one day. It was a lovely and interesting subject to work with."

The Animal Healing film was transmitted, nationwide on Thursday 29th May. Thankfully they put it over very well indeed and gave due credit to Dr Edward Bach showing the dustcover photograph of the good doctor, from *"The Medical Discoveries of Edward Bach Physician."* by Nora Weeks (whom I had come to know so well through some years of corresponding with that amazing lady)

The now famous Rescue Remedy and all the other thirty eight Dr Edward Bach Remedies are obtainable from many health food stores and chemists and a lot of information, books, videos etc, can be obtained from The Bach Centre, Mount Vernon, Sotwell, Wallingford, Oxon OX10 0PZ.

The 'Nationwide' programme heralded "FLOWER POWER" and thankfully put over the subject extremely well, for which I was most grateful and relieved! I take the liberty of quoting the programme now to help widen horizons mentally and spiritually, enabling us to know that there is 'Something Else' far greater than we humans and which supercedes all our known laws and powers.

Luke Casey opened by referring to me as "...a remarkable woman" (but I hasten to say that I am anything but remarkable!) "who lives in the kind of pleasant little road that doesn't exactly scream 'MIRACLE' at you. The sign on the gate though tells you she's different - "No more animals and birds taken in through lack of space and finance".. the back garden is a sort of suburban menagerie with various animals and birds all given up for dead, but all have been cured. She claims to use the Bach Remedies to cure animals. But it is not just the Remedies with Marilyn - she believes in healing for animals, too, and she uses one method or another or a mixture of both, all of which suggests she's a bit of a crackpot, but the extraordinary thing is that whatever Marilyn does for the animals, it seems to work!"

"You don't have to take her word for the cures. All over Devon and Cornwall you will find owners and their pets with reason to thank her. Bruce, the Airedale was only a puppy when he got meningitis. He went blind, deaf, was partially paralysed, and lost his sense of balance. A local vet, called in by his owners, Sybil and Bill Watts, gave the dog every attention, completely exhausting professional veterinary skills. His diagnosis wasn't at all hopeful.
"There was nothing more he could do for him" said Sybil.

"The vet told her there was nothing to lose by bringing Bruce here, but everything to gain."

The interviewer then asked Sybil "How long after you'd taken him to Marilyn did it take him to recover?"
"He could see within two weeks and his balance - he was coming down the stairs - which he couldn't do before. By two weeks he was marvellous!"
"What do you make of it?"

"Well - I believe in it, I am certain it was Marilyn who did the work. I'm convinced it was."

Luke Casey: "So Marilyn's special powers and the Bach Remedies seem to do the trick.. But what are the Remedies? Dr. Bach reckoned it was the cause of the disease you had to work on - not the disease itself. The Remedies were to replace negative thoughts like depression or fear with positive ones."

Luke asked if animals can have negative and positive states of mind as well - and can suffer all these things as we humans do.

"Oh Yes! Exactly the same - they suffer from grief, anger, annoyance; all the things humans suffer, animals can suffer from as well."

"You can't help feeling, that if she lived in the Middle Ages" Luke continued, "Marilyn would be regarded either as a saint or a witch. Nowadays people are more likely to say she's a likeable crackpot and leave it at that. But there's no denying her love for the helpless creatures that find their way to her home. And what about those cures? All those animals now running around happily when the laws of medicine say they should be dead! Coincidence? Or something most of us don't understand yet? All I can say is - if Marilyn Preston is nutty, it's a pity for the world that there isn't more of her kind of madness."

I am not remarkable, neither are the powers of 'mine' - they can be shared by all of us, to be used for the benefit of all life forms. The power can be used negatively to injure or kill - but the karmic debt stands supreme - sooner or later the scales of Universal Justice have to balance and in this life or ones to come, we must reap the results "As ye sow, so must ye reap." Only a few appear to understand what this entails. It involves not just this one little lifetime - we have to take into account what happened before this incarnation and what we are sowing for our future lives. Few realise we have lived before and that we will continue to live on. Nothing and no-one actually dies. What we see left is the cocoon after the butterfly has flown. Where has the 'butterfly' flown beyond our physical sight? To another world which I am sure we can find while still in the physical body, which many appear to have done.

So far I have only glimpsed this Other World but I know without a shadow of doubt that it is REALITY - this world is the shadow, the illusion, though seemingly the real.

In this Other World I have met again my beloved friends, Mr & Mrs Quick, with whom I spent many of my early years and to whom I owe a great deal. Mrs Quick, totally crippled with arthritis 'died' a terrible death in hospital at the age of eighty eight before I knew anything of the Bach Flower remedies. Ernie Quick came to live with Dennis and I and 'died' suddenly but peacefully in my arms four years later. I was devastated and inconsolable. By the time Ernie Quick 'died' I had just understood there was no death but continuous life for all and though it was terribly sad not to be with him any longer, I grieved for my own loss.

It was some time after Mr & Mrs Quick's leaving this world that I found myself with them again in a visionary state. I cannot begin to describe the beauty of where they both were. They met me by a river, where trees and plants, grass and flowers gave off glowing colours far surpassing anything in this world of ours. What thrilled me too were the most beautiful butterflies, large as birds with incandescent wings of the loveliest colours, indescribable in our language though some of my human patients have seen similar things during healing at our home. My old friends were at such peace smiling with happiness and good health. I was sad to leave but happy and joyful too, at there being no sense of worry, anxiety, care, time, physical body or any form of restriction or imprisonment felt in the physical body.

It seems very strange to me that when loved ones go away temporarily it is only natural to keep in touch until we meet again and yet, when they 'die' in this world and go 'abroad' to another world, it is considered bizarre or even wicked or evil to contact them again - what a contradiction.

For the life of me I cannot understand the difference and to my mind and that of a loving God, there must be a way through what we wrongly term 'death'. Indeed there are ways through, one of which Professor Baird Spalding tells in his books *"The Life and Teachings of the Masters of the Far East"* Dr Raymond Moody, in his fine book *"Reunions"* also

71

gives excellent examples of communicating and also actual physical encounters with loved ones who have passed on, including with his own grandmother, long since 'passed on'.

I like to share the words of the world famous teacher Silver Birch, with bereaved folk: *"Do not mourn... Rejoice and know that the enfranchised soul has found liberty and that, if you would unfold the powers that the Great Spirit has given you, you could share some of the new beauty and joy which is theirs."*

But I know only too well the utter grief experienced with the loss of a loved one - human or animal - and it is not easy to carry on living as before. I still find it appallingly difficult despite knowing we all live on and love will draw us all together again.

I share too the words of Bishop Brent; *"We seem to give them back to Thee... who gavest them to us. Yet Thou didst not lose them in giving, so do we not lose them by their return... life is eternal... death is only an horizon... an horizon is nothing save the limit of our sight."*

We do not have to be religious to raise our consciousness to a higher state of being. This world tends to drag us down, it isn't easy to disassociate ourselves and fly higher sometimes to join our Higher Selves, better still, to rejoin our Higher Selves, and live more happily and comfortably here in this world, which is what our main purpose should be! We would see things in an entirely different light should we achieve this reunion, with our True Selves.

Bonny Broadhurst

Following the BBC Nationwide programme a telegram arrived from a Mrs Rita Broadhurst asking for urgent healing help. The telegram asked me to contact her on a STKEVERNE telephone number. Where on earth was Stkeverne? Was it in Norway, Sweden or some far distant place - and how would I get there? I have never flown and don't intend to! I went down to the phone box in the town to ask the operator if she knew which country this far-off place was in. On the point of asking, the penny dropped! It was St. Keverne in Cornwall!

So I rang the number and Peter, the lady's husband answered. They had a Golden retriever in deep trouble with severe hip displasia - at that time incurable. Bonny was almost three when the condition was diagnosed by the vet late in 1975 - both hips were affected and she was limping badly.

Injections had little effect. On the 28th April she had to be carried into the vet's surgery - no mean feat at her weight! Rita and Peter were told nothing more could be done to help Bonny and it would be unfair to let her go on suffering. She was on painkillers but they were told these would produce side effects and might give rise to diabetes.

That very evening Rita remembered she had heard of me doing animal healing - hence the urgent telegram. Next day they all arrived, Peter carrying Bonny in, and we had a fascinating twohours together. Like Freda, Tom and Candy Bowers, I found them a very lovely family. And like them, we have all remained very good friends ever since.

Bonny was brought up for healing once a week through May, June and July but did not visit the vet again. She made slow but steady progress and by summer's end could run once again, which to Rita and Peter was an absolute miracle. They wrote later to say, 'People who have seen this happen are as amazed as we are.'

Later they asked for healing help for a horse called Fantasy, who was suffering from a serious lung condition, was coughing badly and according to the vet had small holes all over her lungs, making breathing difficult, and of course was not able to be ridden. Vets had tried everything to help but nothing further could be done to help Fantasy. As the horse was in another county and I could not get there, absent healing was given, together with one of my 'mental operations' which at that time I had never heard of anyone else doing. I visualised a foam padding around the outside wall of Fantasy's lungs, seeing it as a protective coating through which healing rays streamed inwards.

A week later I was delighted and relieved to hear that Fantasy was being ridden again quite normally, with neither coughing nor breathlessness and a month later a report arrived saying she was absolutely perfect again. It's incredible what the Universal Mind can do!

The story of Bonny and Fantasy is told in Rebecca Hall's marvellous book *'Animals are Equal'* (which was published in 1980 by Wildwood House, and later reprinted by Rider Books).

On the day of publication the BBC in London took an unusual step in making it part of the national six o'clock news. Rebecca was interviewed in the London studio and I was interviewed in the Plymouth BBC TV studio. It was the first time I had taken part in a two-way live television programme and found it quite strange. Watching the small television set before me, I was seeing and listening to Rebecca being interviewed, telling about various animal stories in her book, then I saw another familiar face, though could not quite place it. At that moment I also heard a familiar name running round my head through the headphones.

The 'familiar face' on the screen before me took on a very blank look, which I thought was quite stupid until I realised it was mine! The name was mine as well! The interviewer was talking to me and I was live on television! But my mind had gone totally blank in the confusion, goodness knows what I said! As we didn't have a video in those days I shall never be any the wiser. I fully sympathise now when I see interviewees looking blankly on screen and silence reigning supreme when we are all waiting to hear what they have to say! It's an odd experience.

We have met some wonderful people and animals through the years of healing and have made some lovely friends of many of them, bless them all.

Rebecca has written some excellent books and dramas, and her partner is Gordon F Newman, the writer. We thoroughly enjoyed his two-part BBC drama 'The Healer' some years ago, where a young doctor found he had the gift of healing people and animals - people came in droves with their animals to be healed, but it all got a bit much for the poor chap - and he was not very popular with the hospital staff and his superiors, working miracles with the sick and dying where orthodox treatment was failing! A drama series of Gordon's was launched, with top viewing in 2001 - "Judge John Deed" with Martin Shaw as the Judge. Both Rebecca and Gordon are staunch vegans and seek to spread the word of animal victimisation wherever they can.

There is a postscript to this story which Rita told me about and I think it is intriguing and worth writing about here.

In April 1973 Rita and Pete lost Honey, their much beloved Golden Retriever. She was eleven when she died during an operation and they were left with her sister Sheba. The two dogs had always been with them as they were kept from a litter when they were breeding retrievers. They loved them both but Honey had a very special place in their hearts - she had always been such a character, their pet name for her was HT - short for Holy Terror. She loved the water and as they lived near the sea, had plenty of opportunities for enjoying a swim as well as dips in the river. Another love of her life was her dolly - a soft toy which she loved to carry around.

Rita and Peter were so shaken and sad when she died and both agreed that they couldn't replace her although as is often the case, friends and relations advised them to do this to ease their sense of loss. They decided to carry on as they were; they still had Sheba and fortunately she was in good health.

The weeks passed by after they had made this decision then one day, as Rita was working in the kitchen preparing food for the evening meals, she suddenly felt as though she was being told that they would have Honey back again and as a puppy, and of course she felt a great sense of comfort from this.

Her husband Pete and son Andrew were working outside at the time and she dashed out to them and asked Pete to bear with her if she felt they should get a puppy again after all. He was surprised, but realised she had a strong reason for this and agreed. She felt she had to find out if there was a puppy born at the same time Honey died, so made enquiries with various retriever breeding kennels, but without success, until someone referred her to a place about forty miles from them. She telephoned and was told there were two puppies, both bitches, which were available, as other prospective purchasers at the time only wanted dog puppies. They found that there had only been two in the litter and that they were born in the evening of the same day that Honey had died. Of course, they went to see them and felt immediately that the lighter coloured one of the two must be Honey, however they felt that they shouldn't separate the two sisters, so arranged to buy them both and were allowed to collect them at only five weeks as they had experience of raising puppies.

The pups slept in the car on the way home. When they arrived, Rita and Peter put them down together in the back garden as they got out of the car and suddenly the one they sensed to be Honey started to make a bee-line for the garage. Being so young and tiny, she fell over herself several times, but still plodded on right to the back of the garage, where she stopped and snuffled about. Rita had followed her in, being puzzled at her determination to make for that particular spot, but Pete was amazed as that was exactly where he had hidden Honey's dolly after she died, as he knew if Rita saw it about it would have been more distressing for her. This settled it - they knew she was back with them.

This time they called her Bonny and she and her sister Tansy settled down to life with them and Sheba.

Over the following years they had the usual gladnesses and sadnesses which come with having four-legged members of the family - the most recent sadness was that of Tansy dying during an operation.

As well as their own grief at this they found that Bonny pined for her sister, as you would expect, but then they began to see little changes in her habits of a lifetime. She seemed to be taking on various characteristics of her sister. For instance, Tansy had always enjoyed wading about in the river or in the sea when they took the dogs to the beach, but Bonny was particularly careful not to even get her feet wet, and could only rarely be tempted to the water's edge. They didn't try to change her mind; perhaps she could remember how, as Honey, she had had arthritis for the last few years of her life.

However, the day after Tansy died, they took Bonny to Looe, in Cornwall - they felt they had to get away from the house that day as there was such a dreadful sense of loss, and as they walked on the sands they were extremely surprised to see Bonny make her way straight for the water, where she waded around quite happily! She continued to do that whenever they went near water.

Another thing they found was that Bonny then jumped whenever any wood on the fire crackled or spat and would not stay near the hearth or at times not even in the same room. This, too, was a complete change as she had never taken any notice before - it was always Tansy who reacted in that way. They then had to use a special form of manufactured log so she could enjoy an undisturbed snooze by the fire!

Candy
By Freda and Tom Bowers

Some who brought their companion animals for healing have told their stories in their own words. This is Candy's:

In November 1972 a yellow Labrador joined our family, via the RSPCA. She was fifteen months old, the size of a small pony, with the energy of a wild horse. Throughout the winter she hauled us through muddy fields and woods but gradually we managed to train her, and she settled into three walks a day.

In the spring of 1975 she started standing on three legs, lifting her left back foot off the ground. We took her to the vet who thought at first that she had twisted her knee. The condition rapidly worsened and several x-rays later she was diagnosed as having acute osteo-arthritis - the youngest case the vet had ever seen. A surgeon from the Royal Veterinary College recommended surgery to cut the muscles which would relieve the pain but leave her with a stiff leg. By this time she could only walk about two hundred yards before having to lie down and rest. Her hip joint was visible through the fur - all the flesh seemed to have left her hip. We were at a loss as to what to do.

A chain of events began which could be called coincidence or guidance depending on one's viewpoint. In April we were offered a surprise holiday in a house in Devon. With four days' notice, we were busy getting ready with no time to sit and watch TV after work, but while preparing dinner in the kitchen, I heard a lady being interviewed on BBC Nationwide about her Airedale, which she claimed had been made well by a Healer who "specialised" in helping animals. I dashed to the TV to see who was speaking and just caught the name of the Healer - Marilyn Preston of Saltash in Cornwall. When my hubby came in from the garden, I told him what had happened and we agreed to try and find this lady when we got to Devon: It turned out that Saltash was only twelve miles from our holiday village.

On the Sunday morning we went all over Saltash asking everyone in shops, in the street, anywhere, if they knew of her, and where she lived. We were about to give up when we tried one last shop - yes they knew of her and told us the street where they thought she was living. We eventually found her - and explained our story. She said she would try and help. Candy loves people - any human being is her target for fussing, parading round and round like a circus act, but within a few minutes, Marilyn had her in a deep sleep for about twenty minutes. We had never seen her so quiet. We returned twice more that week and then had to return to Hertfordshire. We noticed some improvement a few weeks later and planned to return to Saltash in September, which we did and Marilyn helped Candy again that week.

During the winter, a definite improvement was obvious. She began to walk further before having to rest. The flesh began to cover the boney hip joint and although she had 'bad' days, most of the time she was much better.

The next year we returned to Devon in the spring, by which time Candy was capable of quite long walks and looked normal around the hip. This was our last personal visit to Marilyn as we bought a Post Office in Derbyshire and it wasn't possible to get to Saltash. However, Marilyn kept Candy in her thoughts and we all kept in touch by letter.

Along with the Post Office we took on a lovely almost white Labrador called Sheba from the previous owners at their request. She was four years old. Although Sheba wanted to be friends with Candy, Candy more or less ignored her, with one exception - Sheba did not like dogs coming near her when she was out for a walk and they usually took her warning growl to heart and left her alone. However if they persisted in teasing her, Candy would see them off in no time, fangs showing and looking fierce.

Sadly, when she was nine, Sheba took ill quite suddenly and within eight days died of a heart attack in my arms. Candy stayed in the lounge for three days, but then behaved quite normally until one Sunday soon afterwards a dog (plus owner), whom she knew, came in the shop and to everyone's astonishment (especially the dog's), Candy turned quite nasty and pinned it in a corner. We had to pull her away. The same thing happened soon afterwards with another dog in the shop; this behaviour only began after Sheba died. It would be wrong to suggest there was any great affection between the two dogs - Sheba often tried to be friends but to no avail. Candy was by far the more dominant personality of the two and Sheba always gave way to her, so that it would be difficult for Sheba to become part of Candy - but the aggressive attitude towards other dogs that Candy now displays in the shop is puzzling - also when she is sound asleep, her face sometimes takes on Sheba's expression.

We will always be so grateful to Marilyn for saving Candy's life for us. She says she didn't do anything - but she is the only person we can see to thank.

Candy is nearly fifteen years old now; she can still walk further than she could before we 'found' Marilyn!

The White Rabbit and the Black Chow

A gentleman who had had a most fascinating healing here for an eye condition, came back later with his wife and their daughter's white paralysed rabbit, asking for healing for the unfortunate creature. The rabbit was a delightful fellow who I felt could be easily healed of whatever was wrong with him, though the vet could do no more. I asked the couple if they would like to leave the rabbit with me and I would give

 him contact healing each day and see how he came along. Snowey had healing twice a day and was very friendly, licking my hand whenever he could. His back half was totally paralysed and he dragged himself around as far as he could by his front legs. Three or four times a day I carried him to the outside sink and holding him against my body depressed his bladder so that he urinated directly into the sink which allowed him to remain clean and dry in his special large indoor box from where he watched all the comings and goings of the house and all the other animals and birds around who lived in our home.

The same week he was brought in, a black Chow was brought in for healing, as he was going blind. The young lady held on to him on a rope as she brought him in, his hackles were up and he was growling fiercely. I could not approach him he was so aggressive, so we sat at opposite ends of the front room as I mentally asked for healing help for him, praying at the same time that he would not slip his collar and take my hand off! Feeling that the healing session had been a complete waste of time, I asked the young lady to let me know if she felt she wanted to bring him back for another session later on, but to make sure she made an appointment beforehand, as was usual with healing sessions. And off they went, the Chow still growling and hackles raised.

Snowey meantime ate well and made friends with all the cats and dogs in the house with Susie the hen, and Piggy the pigeon who also preferred to live indoors rather than outside. I think we also had some injured mice, five baby hedgehogs and three baby swallows who were being hand reared. But Snowey did not seem to be responding to the healing and remained in the same state of partial paralysis.

Two weeks after the 'healing session' with the black Chow, I was shopping in Saltash and going into one particular shop was asked by the lady serving, "Are you Mrs Preston?"
"Yes."
"Well thank you very much for healing my dog the other day."
"What dog was that?"
"The black Chow."
"Oh??"
"Yes, he's fine now thank you - his eyes are cleared of cataracts and he can see perfectly well - and he's a changed character too, and most friendly now."

I was amazed as I never thought anything was happening during the healing at all. A short while later, talking with a friend at a group meeting, I mentioned the incident and she said that she had previously had a court order put on the dog as he was extremely dangerous, having raced out of a house as she was riding by on her horse. He had ripped into the horse's side and hung there by his teeth until the poor horse bolted for about two miles before she could halt him and have his gaping wound seen to by a vet.

Later, when in the fields with my own three dogs, I was even more amazed when the black Chow trotted over to us tail wagging and friendly! What change in the animal!

But sadly, no such wonderful healing occurred with Snowey the lovely, happy, friendly white rabbit. Week after week he remained physically the same and I used to carry him up into the garden where he would 'potter' around in the grass with the other animals during fine days, having his bladder expressed three or four times every day as usual to keep him comfortable, clean and dry.

Then Dennis made him a very handy little trolley on casters which was a marvellous help for Snowey indoors. We would put his body on the trolley and he would use his front legs to pull himself along. Racing up and down the passage into the front room, he would have a chew at the table legs or electric cables or the carpet, then race out again into the kitchen where he would have a nibble at your heels or a chair leg or two. He had all the food he needed of course and some apple tree branches to flex his teeth on, but he preferred better things, causing some dismay and concern, chewing up the house and home! I have a lovely photo of him lying on his stomach as always, holding his front half up with his strong front legs, with Sooty one of our five cats at that time, arm around him, licking his face and with one of her eyes closed in a great wink as if to say "It's alright I'm looking after him."

But just over three years later Snowey was tiring of holding himself up with his forelegs as they were getting deformed with the constant pressure and he kept slipping down again. It must have been terribly frustrating for the dear soul as he did so want to see what was happening from his large, low box where he had to be kept for some parts of the day in the breakfast room. He kept struggling, struggling, struggling to keep up and kept sliding, sliding, sliding down again. At last I found it too painful to bear and decided to call our good vet in to reluctantly put dear Snowey to sleep and out of his struggles.

As we said goodbye to beautiful Snowey and the vet inserted the needle to end his physical life, Snowey licked my hand constantly for the long, long time it took him to pass out of his physical body. Apparently, because of the paralysis the injected euthanaising fluid could not circulate fully and it took much longer than usual. But Snowey was quiet and apparently content during the whole of this time until he finally succumbed, with his tongue still licking my hand until it stopped there and he slid quietly over onto his side, at peace at last.

Both the vet and I were in tears and mine were dropping onto the perfectly white still body of beloved Snowey. The dogs came over to say goodbye in their turn, then the cats. The vet took his leave and I lit a candle for my departed little friend and placed a flower in a small vase by his head, saying a prayer for his freedom and happiness now and thanks for the love he shared with us all. I would bury his body in the garden on the third day.

The next day I felt impressed to visit one of the Spiritualist Churches in Plymouth for a service. After the service followed 'readings' by a clairvoyant (clairvoyant means clear vision: clairaudient means clear hearing). I was surprised when the medium pointed to me saying "I'm coming to the lady in the back there. I don't know if you understand this but there is the most beautiful Persil-white rabbit here with me, standing on his hind legs and reaching up to my waist. He's asking me to thank you for everything you have done for him. Does this make sense to you?"

With tears flowing down my face and a lump in my throat I tried to say "Yes it does - thank you!" I did not know if she ever heard me…

No amount of money in the world could have done as much for me as that moment in time when Snowey came back to say thank you… What wonderful proof of our beloved animal friend's survival after 'death'. I was completely unknown in that church and to that person. No-one knew anything about Snowey and I certainly did not go expecting to have such a revelation. It does change one's sadness to joy to know they are fine, well and happy, waiting 'just round the corner' 'til we meet again.

But what a paradox with the white rabbit and the black Chow. There was no love lost between the Chow and me and he had a miraculous healing, both with his sight and his nature. With all the love in the world between Snowey and me, and all the many, many, healings he was given he remained partially paralysed until the day he 'died' but then he was healed for his new life, thank God.

It doesn't seem that 'love' is the answer to healing, not as we see it, anyway, at the moment.

Postscript:

They say that truth is stranger than fiction and sometimes it is!

The day after I wrote this story down a lady came for her first healing appointment, and during her healing we talked of a mutual love of the animal kingdom.

She began telling me about a 'big black Huskie dog' she befriended some years ago in this town. He was almost continually chained up outside a house and being the target of stones and bottles etc. "Everyone was terrified of him" she told me. But he loved her and waved his tail, curled over his back, whenever he saw her coming along the road. She began buying him meat and giving him bones whilst talking to him, as a loving bond developed between them. His name, she found, was Budeaux and she constantly worried about the poor chap, out in all weathers, often finding him wound round by his chain, hardly able to move.

Circumstances changed and the lady and her family moved away.

One morning Budeaux was found, still chained, but battered to death, with blood everywhere. The lady was horrified when she heard and most dreadfully upset. After all Budeaux had gone through and to end his life like this! It was too much and many tears flowed for him.

About two years later the good lady went to a large hall in a nearby town which was packed with folk wanting to hear from loved ones who had passed on. The 'sensitive' honed in on this kind soul and said to her that there was a 'big, black, fierce Huskie dog' by her side, protecting her.

She was immediately aware that it was dear Budeaux and the knowledge gave her much upliftment as she thought he was 'dead and gone'. And as you will have guessed by now, Budeaux was the Black Chow! It seems that after his healing when his cataracts disappeared and he became much friendlier creature, more ill-treatment caused him to return to his wary, fearful nature of old, which is hardly surprising. He became defensive and began to attack again, trusting no-one but his friend, until at last he suffered a terrible ending to his physical life.

But how wonderful that the Black Chow made his presence known to the kindly soul who loved him, albeit two years after leaving this dimension of life, and the White Rabbit, Snowey, made his presence known to me the very next day after passing from his physical body!

Thor and Dennis

One day back in 1971 the kind RSPCA Inspector called - he had a bit of a problem. A very oiled swan was sitting in a sack in his van, looking fiercely disgruntled and hostile. The Inspector's problem was what to do with him and I offered to take him on in our tiny Wild Bird and Animal Hospital here (which is now closed after many years of running on my own).

He carried the large bird in the sack up to the pen at the top of the garden and slipped the sack off. The swan stood his ground and hissed at us both, wings uplifted menacingly. The Inspector then joined me in a cup of coffee in the house and finally asking if I was sure it was alright to leave the swan with me, took his leave saying he would be back if I couldn't cope. I was sure there would be no trouble at all.

Finding the largest Pyrex dish in the kitchen I filled it with a dozen and one things I thought a swan would be tempted to try, all arranged in neat piles to see what would be gobbled up first. Aware that a strike with a swan's wing could break an arm or leg I approached him quietly and very slowly, holding the dish well out in front of me towards him - would he be hungry and gratefully take the offering?

With a great Hiss a wing shot up and came down with full force on the proffered dish. It shattered in half and everything lay in a mess as he glared at it, then at me with anger and defensiveness. I don't know who was the more frightened - him or me? With a sinking heart I wondered how on earth to tackle this, my first swan patient. Somehow I had to get him into the house, up the stairs to the bathroom to give him a thorough cleaning and wash. But HOW?

Going into the pen I sat down a little distance from him and spoke to him explaining that somehow or other we had to trust each other otherwise there was no way I could possibly help him. Putting out my hand to him very cautiously and slowly, he suddenly reached forward taking the back of my hand by the skin and ferociously tearing at it with his sharp beak. Keeping it there I allowed him to see that I intended him no harm but sending him thoughts that I wanted to help him in his distress and plight.

For an hour or so he kept up his defences.

Then suddenly the flash went out of his eyes. The glare softened his body relaxed and his head lowered. In that instant I knew I could trust him and he knew he could trust me. We were friends! With thankfulness I put my arm around his back and he, joy of joys, put his neck round mine as I sat with him on the ground. Clearing up the broken glass and food I put it in the bin wrapped in newspaper and began to prepare the next biggest thing in which to put some food, a washing-up bowl.

After he had picked over some of the food I stayed talking with him and gaining his confidence before telling him he was about to be tucked under my arm and taken for a walk - up into our bathroom for a clean up.

Thankfully this was accomplished without much ado, although it took several changes of warm, soapy bathwater to get him looking anywhere near clean again. Then I discovered he had an injured leg and looked very sorry for himself.

When Dennis came home from work and saw the bathroom door shut he asked "Why?"
"'Cos there's a little bird in there who needs to be kept quiet!" His expletive is unrepeatable here, when he went up and opened the door! He got used to it after a few months and took it for granted that Thor the swan got tucked under my arm in the mornings for the trip downstairs and up into the garden to the grass and his paddling pool, with the return trip in the evenings to the newspaper strewn

bathroom to spend the night as he was not waterproofed at this time unfortunately. By the time I had seen to all the other animals and bird patients here it was time to have my bath, usually around one or two in the morning. Thor and I would spend half-an-hour or so honking gently to each other and gently relaxing from the rigours of the day.

Thor took a long time to make any headway and I had a very strong feeling that he had lost his mate and found it very hard going on his own. Swans mate for life and it is distressing for them to lose a mate - so very much like humans and some other animals and birds.

In the nine months he was here with us his main diet was masses of lettuce, saffron cake and cheese which I found he cared for more than any of the many other foods I tried with him. He then became restless and we realised it was time for him to return to the wild. Dennis and I took him out to Moditonham Quay near Saltash where a friend lived and where he was first found in such a sad state. We released him on the river there and said our goodbye's to him, wishing him well.

We tried to keep track of him to know how he was faring as previously we had taken him to a friend at Ashburton for further recuperation but after a week he had flown off and had to be rescued and brought back here again.

Through the Sunday Independent newspaper and the Western Evening Herald we found that he had 'emigrated ' to Torpoint in Cornwall and he became quite well known there, as he never lost his limp from his injured leg.

A year or so later on Christmas Eve at about ten o'clock in the evening we had an urgent police message - there was a swan in trouble at Torpoint. Could we investigate please? Knowing I could not settle, Dennis kindly drove me over but all the swans seemed alright on the high tide and we eventually returned home again.

Three days later, another urgent message came and a friend dashed me over in her car. This time I saw Thor lying on the beach in a terrible state, unable to hold his head up properly and breathing with much difficulty. He was in serious trouble and had been washed in and out by the tides each day.

Calling his name I ran to him with tears pouring down my face - to find tears trickling down his face also and dropping off his lowered beak.

Gathering him in my arms I placed his soft neck around mine as we used to do and we all drove home in quietness. The earthly end was near for my friend.

I carried dear Thor up into the bathroom and prepared some of his favourite food but he was unable to eat anything. He tucked his head over his back and slept...

The following evening at ten o'clock Thor quietly and peacefully died in my arms. With a huge ache in my heart and lump in my throat I prayed to the Supreme Intelligence that Thor would now be reunited with his true mate and find peace, freedom and happiness at last, in his continuing life.

All forms of life live on in other vibrations, other dimensions, other worlds, some interplaning with our own Earth plane.

Next morning Dennis and I drove with Thor's white body to return it to the wild again. We placed it lovingly on the fast flowing high tide up a little used estuary near St. Germans, his neck laid gracefully along his back, and we quietly watched as the waters took him away and eventually beached him on a grass plateau. We returned home in sombre silence, neither of us able to speak.

One evening four years later I was stunned to find Dennis had quite suddenly left his earthly body too - sitting in his chair just a few minutes after we had been talking about animal healing.

It must be a wonderful way to go Home, to go to sleep in one world and awaken in another.

At his semi-military funeral, the weather was grey and drizzling. After the service, taken by an army padre and a spiritualist minister, both friends of ours, we came to the graveside unable to see more than a few yards through the gloom.

A bugler, one of Dennis's former army cadets and now with his battalion at Shrewsbury, sounded the Last Post. As the last deeply moving notes died away in the still, misty air, a beautiful shaft of Light came down piercing the gloom and lit up the scene.

I felt a sudden sense of awe and looked up into the light expecting to see an Angel, but could see nothing. Several mourners also looked up - what were they expecting? Then three of them came to me in turn asking me if I had seen what was in the extraordinary beam of light.

Each described a BEAUTIFUL WHITE SWAN WITH OUTSTRETCHED WINGS over my head.

That is why you will find Thor carved on Dennis's headstone today. And this is why I am writing this book now - because Thor asked me to tell his story and that of some animals and birds who have sought sanctuary here over the years before I had to close. One day I hope Thor will tell his own story.... as Jonathan Livingston Seagull did to the writer Richard Bach - and what an amazing and wonderful story that is!!

The Long Dark Night of the Soul

The days following the death of my husband Dennis were a blur, with a total sense of unreality. So very many things had to be done and friends and family were a great help, thankfully, as there is no way I could have coped on my own, with all the various things which have to be done at such a critical time. One seems to be on autopilot and you somehow get through the days doing things which must be done. Especially with animals and birds to be cared for all the time, you simply keep going. I began to eat a little cheese, and an egg now and then, when affordable and whilst I had been very fit and active, needing little sleep all those years as a vegan, the diet changed to vegetarianism.

However, within the next two months two other major traumas followed and I was left a wreck, waking each morning under a black cloud of despair and hopelessness and not knowing which way to turn. 'The goal' I had kept in mind for all that time, vanished in the thickening gloom.

For nine months I dreaded the post arriving each day as I was expecting to lose my home. Where would I go with some fifty birds and animals? My nerves were in such a state I could not leave the house for nearly a year. A kindly neighbour took my three rescued dogs out each day for a walk and friends kindly did the shopping for me. With only £9 (or was it £11 then?) a week widow's pension, there was very little to buy food with, with all the bills to be paid and animals and birds to be fed. It was an ongoing nightmare.

In all these years we have never charged for healing, but on some occasions people have very kindly insisted on leaving a donation and this has been of tremendous help, especially after Dennis died, when often I did not know where the next meal was coming from. And since then, often when a bill, such as the telephone, has awaited payment, donations have miraculously materialised, thankfully!

It is only when one goes through a long dark night of the soul that one can really understand what it is like for others. There are times when it is utterly impossible to 'pull yourself up by your bootlaces' no matter how well-meaning some people are when they say this. They have never 'been there' or felt the utter and deepest anguish of the soul. It is only recently that I have come to realise that often this depression is caused by a chemical deficiency in the brain caused by a lack of serotonin, through grief, stress, worry and other emotional traumas.

Unfortunately, I could find nothing to help along 'natural' lines of treatment having tried everything I came across although many others have found such help, I know. Healing did not help either except one night, in the depths of despair when after feeding all the animals, I took two very strong sleeping tablets and a glass of whisky, which I can't stand, intending to go to bed to sleep, sleep, sleep. Then I walked (wombled would be a better description) out of the house and down the road to the town and vaguely made out the telephone box set in the wall of the Post Office. Hands in pockets, I felt my fingers wrap around the two penny piece in one pocket. That's it! phone my Irish healer friend, Maureen!

I had no idea until later that it was gone midnight but Maureen said she was coming to meet me - I headed for the bottom of the town to start the long descent down the road to her home. A lone figure came towards me and I barely remember any more until sitting in her lounge with a cup of black coffee in very wobbly hands. Maureen then gave me healing with a lovely prayer, I remember. She said that as I slowly moved towards her coming down the street I was leaning on 'Someone'. A few minutes after the healing, life and peace came pouring into me so that by about one thirty in the morning I was able to get up, fully recuperated and walk up the long hill and the main street alone and home to bed, walking on air! It was quite amazing healing! No way these days would I be out at night, alone and completely unafraid.

However, some weeks later, one night, on the point of suicide, my five cats and three dogs surrounded me in the breakfast room. With the chosen knife in my hand I looked at them all as they gazed unblinking at me. Then my Inner Voice spoke quietly, explaining that if I left them now it would take hundreds of earth years for me to atone to them for the distress it would cause them; I was to hang on and wait for help to come. I put the knife away in the kitchen drawer, hugged all the creature friends and broke my heart again. All I wanted was oblivion, but it was apparent that suicide was not the way out of anything unfortunately. However I can understand anyone who does take their own life, and have sympathy for them if they find themselves in an appalling situation, through no fault of their own and no way out. Some are so grief stricken they cannot bear to go on alone, I can empathize with that.

After nine nerve-racking months I learned I could keep the house and on that morning went up into the garden somewhat brighter, to hang out the washing. As I was pulling up the clothes line suddenly the wooden clothes -pole gave an almighty groan and came crashing down - right through the greenhouse which was my 'bird-nursery' in the Spring and which was sheltered from the sun. Sitting down among the shattered glass I wept and wept.

The house was in an awful state as the roof leaked in several places, there was no damp course and being an end-terraced house with cracks throughout the end wall all the rooms were damp. Nails were keeping some of the window panes in and I dreaded the southerly gales which rattled and shook the panes to breaking point - towels soaked up some of the rain coming in, but the rest trickled down the walls. Now the garden looked as though a bomb had hit it!

With no more tears to cry, sitting among the glass, wet clothes draped over the aviaries and seagull's pen, I began to pray and ask for help, if there was any available. Could God or whoever it was 'up there' please help to find someone to come into my life to somehow get me up out of this nightmare, someone who could tolerate me, all the faults and failings, beliefs and way of life? All these birds and animals, life on other dimensions, spaceships, vegan/vegetarianism, continuing life after death. The request went out from the depths of my soul as I asked that if there was that special person who would be right for me and even more importantly that I would be right for him, that somehow or other we could be brought together for our mutual benefit. Was there such a person on the planet?

Starting to clear up the glass I felt I had passed my great burden over to Higher Hands and some peace began to creep into my weary mind and body.

An Old Gentleman

One autumnal evening in 1978 I had gone by bus to the Plymouth home of Barney and Mary Camfield for healing when a gentleman gave me healing and some peace of mind. Whilst waiting at the bus stop for the journey home I saw a bent, elderly man coming up the steps dressed in an old army greatcoat and with a flat cap on his head. He looked into the rubbish bins, obviously hoping to find something edible but was disappointed and trudged on.

He then proceeded down the opposite set of steps as my bus was coming into the station and I walked down the steps he had come up, thinking how could I help him? Having enough money in my pocket for the return journey there was just one pound coin left. Holding it, I bent down as though I had just picked it up from the ground as the old gentleman was about to pass by me. Holding it out to him I simply said "Perhaps you could do with this more than I can at the moment?"

I have never seen a face light up so much for so little. With a beautiful smile on his careworn face which I can still see now, a single tooth showing he took his hand out of his deep packet, saluted and said "God bless you ma'am I only have this one penny for a couple of days!" and he opened his other hand to show it to me.

Getting on my bus I watched him as he walked away, with head and shoulders now up, and my heart sang for him.

On going to bed that night I prayed one of the deepest prayers of my life, asking for help and blessings for the old man and those like him who had no food or drink and perhaps no roof over their head, for those who were **really** 'down and out'. Sobbing for those who had nothing I cried myself to sleep, my beloved animal friends around me.

Next morning I awoke to an incredibly different world! I felt light and very, very happy, something not felt for many years. Looking out of the window I found the rooftops appeared to be shining. The pavements were shining too with a light not seen before. People came into view, how were they shining too? And laughing! What on earth was happening? Why was I so happy? I felt no longer alone but as though someone wonderful was with me, companioning me. Coming downstairs I fed all the animals, then the birds in the aviaries and pens. They all looked so different - they were shining also - and I was filled with the utmost happiness similar to the short time when I met my Space Friend from another world.

As the day progressed so did the inner happiness. Where was it all coming from? I wasn't on any treatment from my doctor or anything else - I had given up any hope of help at that time having tried so many things. The face of the old gentleman at the bus station repeatedly came into my mind.

I had been attending meditation evenings for a while, (with a friend who had a car), at the home of Dr. Alec Forbes a consultant physician who recognised the benefits that Spiritual Healing can provide.

At the meditation with Dr Forbes I was filled with such happiness that it brimmed over everywhere and he had to call me to order, requesting all of us to 'centre' ourselves, but having been depressed for so long, I wanted to enjoy this new sense of living to the full and not come to my 'centre'. Not yet anyway!

Friends came to see me, and some people and animals for healing, and everything went amazingly well with wonderful results on many occasions. My 'Companion' remained with me and the happiness increased so much that I had to ask to be given no more or I would burst with it!! For six days and nights the total bliss and joy was almost too much to bear. What a tremendous difference from the darkness of the long night of the soul previously gone through. I felt I had been uplifted to a new plane of life, which I already knew existed of course and on which plane people can live in their higher consciousness. THIS WAS REALLY LIVING! If only all earthly life forms could feel like this all the time - it would indeed be Heaven on Earth! I was so very grateful for this beautiful feeling and the Presence within.

In the early hours of the next morning I suddenly awoke knowing someone wanted me. I lay in bed wondering who it was…waiting. The doorbell rang and I put on my dressing gown going down the stairs to answer the door. (Would we dare do such a thing these days I wonder if living alone?). A chap I knew was on the doorstep. "Please can you come to help my mother, Mrs Preston? She is in agony and the morphine she's on does not help now." I got dressed and we drove to the home of the elderly lady.

She was indeed in a great deal of pain with a terrible wound in her leg into which one could have put the first joint of one's thumb, the bone being visible as she took off the heavy dressing applied daily by a District Nurse. I can never promise a cure, of course, as the results of healing are not in our hands. One is simply a channel for the Healing Intelligence, which obviously knows full well what It is doing!

Talking with the lady whilst giving healing to her leg and mentally requesting help for the condition and for the lady herself, it was noticeable she was very resentful of certain things and I allowed her to continue to talk, to 'get it all out'. After a while, looking down at her leg, I was shocked to see movement in the deep hole and had to force myself to look closer. Yes - something was moving in there! I had to steel myself to try to find out what it was. With amazement I realised it was new flesh actually GROWING! It began to fill the hole as we watched - as though many weeks of new, clean flesh was growing in the space of as many minutes! Having seen many other miracles happening during healings, perhaps I should not find it so amazing but it was! As the patient continued talking I found myself empathizing with her and my own inner feelings became somehow distorted and began 'sinking'.

All the happiness began to fade and I suddenly became fully aware of the Presence which had been with me for the past six days and nights, walking out of the door of the room. I silently called out, begging It to return but it was gone and I felt totally alone again.

With heart as heavy as lead I also took my leave and was driven home again. The world and everything had returned to 'normal', sadly. But I have been privileged to know that the Kingdom of Heaven is within and is here - if we can but find it!

Later when a friend kindly sent me a copy of *'A Course in Miracles'* I was to learn that we are supposed to 'rise above the battlefield' but I came right down into it with the elderly patient's resentments and lost it all!

Also when James Redfield's best seller *'The Celestine Prophecy'* was published in 1993 it gave me further insight into what had happened on that sixth evening. The group had learned that we are meant to reach Heaven on Earth whilst we are still here, and that when people raise their vibrations to such a level that it appears everything is shining with a glowing from within, and then to a state where others cannot see them, it signals that we are crossing the barrier between this life and the other world to which we go after death

The group was then approached by soldiers but to their amazement they realised they could not be seen by the men who were searching for them because they were 'vibrating too highly'. Then they found that two other men from the group had been captured, which jolted them, and their energy plummeted in their concern and fear for their friends. The senior group leader shouted to them to wait and not to lose their energy, but through 'descending into the battlefield' they had lost their power and were now seen by the soldiers and captured.

We are supposed to 'maintain a sufficient vibration in all situations', but how do we do just that? I most certainly lost 'my vibration' to my deep regret, when empathising with the resentful elderly lady whose leg was almost healed by the time I left her home. And I still frequently fall into the trap to this day. But one day we shall all get 'There'!

Rescued!

It was not until over a year later that my prayer was answered. I received a letter from an old friend Dennis and I had known several years before, asking if he, Frederick could call and visit me for a couple of days the following weekend, he would be coming on his own. We had originally met him and his family through a strange encounter with a black Labrador spirit dog belonging to a friend of theirs.

Some considerable time after that first meeting, I became seriously ill with pleurisy and quinsy in my throat and being a staunch anti-vivisectionist and opposed to anything coming from animal experimentation at that time I was refusing to have a doctor, an operation or any medical treatment.

Dennis thought I was going to die as I could neither eat nor drink anything for a week and by that time I too thought I was, every minute was agony! My husband insisted I write a letter to my parents explaining my decision and that if I died it was not **his** fault as he wanted me to have the doctor. They were very concerned and in their urgent reply asked me to have medical help.

The next day was a Sunday and I heard the front door bell ring and the sound of voices. A short while later Dennis and Frederick came into the bedroom. I was far from pleased that we had visitors. I could not speak and Frederick's wife and daughter were downstairs. I did not know until years later that Dennis had telegrammed Frederick to please come to give me healing, as he was a very good healer and my husband was getting desperate.

I was taken downstairs somehow or other and put on a chair in the dining room (as it then was - today it is the study). Dennis left Frederick and I to join Joan and Debbie in the lounge.

What happened then was absolutely amazing.

Standing somewhere behind me, Frederick commenced channelling healing to and for me. I was aware of a small round 'cap' being placed on top of my head and gradually, very gradually an anaesthetised effect spread from the cap downwards over my forehead, eyes, ears, nose, mouth, chin and neck until it reached the top of both shoulders where it stopped in a straight line. If Frederick had put say a large knitting needle right through my neck, I would not have felt it of that I was quite certain.

Then a beautiful 'blast' of warm air came through my back into my chest considerably easing the pain and distress of trying to breathe.

I completely forgot Frederick at this point as although I could not physically see it I became aware of a machine of some sort being taken from somewhere on my left to be placed immediately in front of me. Suddenly two white 'laser beams' of light came from the machine and begun slicing through the quinsy, a peritonsillar abcess, which appeared to have solidified, blocking my throat completely. The slices dropped down my throat and I wondered what on earth they looked like. The 'laser beams' switched off, my throat was clear and the machine was taken back again to somewhere on my left side.

Another blast of warm air came into my back and circulated round inside my chest, which felt marvellously soothing and healing. Gradually, very gradually the anaesthetic was 'lifted up' until it finally reached the little round 'cap on my head. (The 'cap' stayed for a couple of days after the healing).

I heard Frederick's voice coming from behind me - "How are you feeling now?" Swallowing, then taking a deep breath I found I was totally healed. I could walk alright on my own too! Going into the lounge Dennis was amazed that I was fine and I was able to talk to Joan and Debbie quite normally. When we all sat down to tea it was as though I would never stop eating and drinking.

It was an absolute miracle - friends who came the following day to carry on feeding, watering and generally looking after all the birds and animals were equally amazed as I don't think they expected to see me again!

Back to the beginning of this chapter; answering the letter I said it would be nice to meet him again, but I was in a terrible state, very depressed and no company for anyone. Perhaps it would be better if he didn't come…

On the Friday evening Frederick arrived expecting something to eat! Being so low I rarely even thought about food for myself let alone a guest. So we had to go out shopping for something to cook. After the meal we talked.

He had gone to the Dr. Edward Bach Centre, to have a talk with the then curator, Mrs Nickie Murray, needing some direction in his life. Nickie 'just happened' to mention my name to Frederick who replied "Oh, I know Marilyn and Dennis Preston!" She then told him Dennis had passed on early in 1977 and I was in a state to which he said that he had been divorced less than a year later and had no idea that Dennis had died.

That evening he decided to write me to see if he again could give some healing to help me. Hence his letter, and that is how my heartfelt prayer for help was answered from above, thankfully. We were married three years later. Little did I realise, just after we first met all those many years ago, when coming out of their home in Bude with Dennis one Sunday, and The Voice had said to me "You will be working with him one day" and to which I had immediately replied that there was no way I wanted to work with him, thank you, that we would end up years later, married!

Since then we have worked together giving healing to humans and animals alike, though of course there was little time for him to join me in that whilst he had to work so hard and long until retiring on the state pension a few years ago.

'Upstairs' had planned all that many moons ago, quite obviously, for which I give deepest thanks for such a lovely soul to have come into my life. Not only has Frederick rescued me, but also the old house which was crumbling round my ears. He is still rescuing me even today.

'The Wild Animal Woman'

It had been pouring with rain all day, the wind playing havoc with everything not battened down, howling and swirling the dead leaves in whirlpools of bits and pieces of everything it could find to play with.

But it was Friday and scrubbing out day in the aviaries so it had to be done as this was the day of the week I had organised myself to do this for many years and I was getting fed up with the continual chore, I must say.

The winters I dreaded most, when, aching with the cold and my hands and feet numb, I would often cry with pain - never could stand the cold at the best of times!

With wellies and waterproofs on plus rubber gloves I was busily cleaning down the path and steps with all the accumulated rubbish from the pens and aviaries, and having lost my rain hat my hair was soaking wet and being blown around in an increasing mess - not a pretty sight!

Becoming aware of the dogs barking in the house I realised the front doorbell must be ringing, so dropped tools and hurried into the house, trailing rivulets of water behind me. Opening the front door, I stood there, a picture of well groomed elegance, looking at the lady waiting expectantly outside it. I must say she looked a trifle taken aback at the sight before her eyes, but she nevertheless managed to ask "Are you the wild animal woman?"

It appears she had found a wild animal and it was in her car and please would I take it in?

It was not until later I realised how appropriate her question really was! After falling about laughing for a while I pulled myself together to see to the waif and stray just brought in.

At that time I had been writing personally to the Editor of the Spiritual Healing Magazine, Terry Neuman, who I found had a terrific sense of humour and I would often howl with laughter as his letters unfolded such wit as well as the deeper, spiritual matters of life which were so important to us and so many thousands of others. I was awaiting one of

Terry's letters any day, when he had the time in his very busy life to reply to my last one.

However, I thought the Wild Animal Woman story too good to keep to myself, so I sent it as a letter to be printed in the Sunday Express, which was duly printed the following Sunday.

In those days we had Sunday collections from Post Offices and delivery of same on the Monday morning.

We were still chuckling over my printed story in the Sunday Express when the post arrived on Monday morning. Among the dozens which arrived for me (I used to reply to about a hundred a week on animal welfare, the anti-vivisection work in which I was closely engaged and healing matters), was one addressed simply to

The Wild Animal Woman

Saltash

Cornwall

With a puzzled brain I opened the envelope and guess who it was from? Yes friend Terry had found it irresistible too, when he saw the story in the paper and the good souls at our local Post Office didn't have too much of a guess to realise who the addressee was. How's that for service? Not a very becoming title I must admit, but an unusual one!

Lassie

Lassie had been brought to us via Plymouth Police, just six months after the 'death' of our beloved Panda and Kim back in 1968. After a year, we found that when she came into season life became extremely difficult. She must have had a most divine scent because all the dogs of the neighbourhood came tearing round and sat panting outside the house day and night for several days at the height of the exciting time. Then they started leaping over the garden wall, oblivious to the 8ft drop on the other side.

Three of us, with sticks at the ready, had to stand guard over her each time we ventured out in the garden for her to spend a penny whilst a variety of dogs, including the old faithfuls, milled around.

To go out shopping on my own I had to spray myself with a dog deterrent (which smelt dreadful) and one day found myself trapped by two large dogs and unable to reach home at all. Eventually, managing to get to a friend's house on the way, I asked if her husband could act as my bodyguard to get home in one piece. I may say it's somewhat embarrassing having to have an escort with a hefty walking stick and being followed by a growing trail of dogs all the way home.

So the decision was reached, that Lassie would have to be spayed, something which had been put off as a friend's dog had died under the anaesthetic for such an operation. However it was subsequently found she had a very weak heart. It was a most unusual case and rarely happens but I was still worried, such operations were more difficult to perform then than they are today with more modern equipment and anaesthetics.

The evening before Lassie was due to be spayed I spoke at length with a doctor in the spirit world at a Plymouth spiritualist church. It seemed that Dr Chang was a kindly soul and very knowledgeable. He was very fond of birds and animals so we got along fine. I asked if someone in the spirit world could operate on Lassie so that she would not have to have the physical operation but Dr Chang explained that there were many things we had to do for ourselves in this physical world and added "You will be shown tonight whether it will be alright or not."

I waited all evening for him to come back to tell or show me whether things would be 'alright or not'. But he did not and the healer came out of trance without my being able to have a word with Dr Chang again. Very disappointed I came home.

Going to sleep, I suddenly found myself leaving my body - being 'transported' to a most lovely field with the sun shining and the air beautifully clear and still. Waiting, I was then aware of two dogs bounding in great joy and happiness towards me - Panda and Kim! Overjoyed with being able to see them, touch them and play with them again, my heart was overwhelmed with gratitude. They were both the picture of health and vitality - so vastly different from their appearance just before 'death' when they were extremely, painfully, distressingly ill. Here they now were, more keenly alive and happy than when on the earthly plane. They bounded with pure joy of living and were as delighted at being with me again, as I was at being with them. I longed to have a pair of scissors to cut some wool from Panda's coat, to simply prove to people that here I was, actually with them, knowing no-one would believe me without such proof. Unfortunately the scissors were not forthcoming and I could not tug even the tiniest amount of wool from her coat.

Then a strange thing, she then stood side-on to me, waiting. As I looked there was a new spaying operation scar on the side of her body, in a newly shaved area. Yet only cats are spayed on the side, bitches are operated on up through the middle of the tummy underneath. I asked what it meant and was mentally told that it was just to show me about the spaying operation as it applied to Lassie the next morning. I asked if Lassie would be alright and the scar disappeared from Panda's side and she dashed off to play like a two year old. Yes everything would be alright for Lassie as it was being shown to me through Panda's reaction.

Panda, Kim and I walked and larked around for a while longer and then it was morning and time to get out of bed. I now had no worries about Lassie and realised, so that was Dr Chang's meaning when he said the evening before, that I would be shown that night whether it would be alright or not and it had to be shown me on Panda's side as I could not have seen the operation if it was done in the normal place.

We took Lassie to the veterinary surgeon that morning for the operation which was to take place at eleven o'clock. We had been promised we could have her back by the evening, but I could ring at lunchtime to find out how the op. went. This I did and was delighted to hear the vet say we could come out any time and pick her up as all was fine.

Dennis and I borrowed my brother's Rover car as it would be nice and roomy enough to put a box on the floor-space at the back and build up the back seat, and over this to form a big bed to place our collie cross on as she would still be anaesthetised. Our 'ambulance' now ready we belted along to the surgery.

But what was that we heard when we there? A familiar bark rang out again and again; it could not be Lassie could it? Leading the vet out of the waiting room door came Lassie to greet us, glassy-eyed and staggering somewhat, but nevertheless making a beeline for us. How she knew it was us and in an unfamiliar car we didn't know, Telepathy? All the way there my thoughts were with her and beaming out the message "We're on our way to bring you home Lassie!" She obviously got the message!

The kindly vet explained he was amazed, especially as he said he 'had to use dynamite to do the operation' because of fat which had built up around the area though she was not fat outwardly.

107

Thankfully Lassie never looked back and made a fine recovery, but I had already been shown that all would be well and perhaps Dr Chang and his spirit helpers worked with the vet so that all went especially well - I don't know as he never did tell me.

In 1980 when Lassie was twelve years old she suffered four strokes and for a while was totally blind. In one of the drastic stages she fell from top to bottom of a long flight of stairs and was terrified. Giving her frequent doses of the Dr Edward Bach Flower Remedies she gradually came to and her sight returned to a limited extent. It was obvious that she also needed urgent veterinary help and this was given, though we all had grave doubts whether she could survive. However, with the help of the excellent vets, the Dr Edward Bach Flower Remedies together with healing, Lassie was able to walk and to be active again, although after the fall down the stairs she never attempted to go upstairs again. Despite this she was always ready for her walks in the park or the fields every day with Hattie.

Hattie had been brought to us by Saltash Police in April 1976 having been abandoned at Hatt, near Saltash as a pup of about six weeks of age, suffering badly from diarrhoea and a variety of things all of which thankfully responded naturally and well. She was so poorly at first that we decided to keep her for a week at least until better and then try to re-home her. But she crept into our hearts and ended up, like so many other creatures, staying with us despite the fact that often we had to live on odds and ends as all the housekeeping was swallowed up with the animal and bird food bills. Often I would go to bed in tears, wondering how on earth to get through the following day.

By the age of seventeen Lassie was becoming extremely frail and her vision more restricted. On Mothering Sunday 1985 she became very distressed early in the morning and her sight went altogether, again. The Rescue remedy restored it within an hour or so, to the tunnel vision, but it was obvious that we would have to make a decision on her future. After a long, serious talk Frederick and I decided it would be kinder to have Lassie gently put to sleep as life was getting more and more difficult for her. She had also been incontinent for quite a while which can be most distressing for a sensitive animal. It is not much fun for the 'owners' either! I speak from good experience, having had Laddie, a totally incontinent dog for eight years.

At eleven o'clock on that Sunday morning, Mothering Sunday, a kind vet arrived with his assistant and at eleven thirty a needle slid into Lassie's leg. Her head sank slowly to the ground and before the needle was withdrawn she had breathed her last breath in this lifetime on this dimension. It is always very sad and moving when a friend leaves, sometimes more so with an animal friend. We prayed she would be fine now, free and happy, and the tears flowed. Her golden coloured body stayed all that day, in her favourite place in the breakfast room looking peaceful and content, her eyes with a far away look.

That evening just before going to bed I was breaking my heart on Frederick's shoulder in the kitchen. Mentally I then pulled myself together and silently asked "Please let me know, if you can, that Lassie is alright now?" Instantly the cats leapt off their chairs and dashed out through the cat flap in the door. Rushing after them I opened the door to see what all the commotion was about and lo and behold, over our house was the most beautiful shooting star I have ever seen, its tail a myriad of stars.

"Look there goes our Lassie!" I immediately cried to Frederick and knew that it was a given sign that she was indeed fine and away to freedom. I glanced at the clock, it was eleven thirty that night, twelve hours to the minute after Lassie was released from her seventeen year old physical overcoat, her body.

She had been such a gentle dog and had wanted to mother any little animal or bird which had been brought in over the many years and none of them was frightened of her interest and care, not even the tiniest fledgling. It took me a long time to realise the telepathic communication between the members of the animal kingdom, something with which we humans have not as yet caught up. When she was first brought to us Lassie saved us from a severe fire in one of the

109

bedrooms by literally pulling me into the bedroom and taking me to the bed where I found it smouldering from a faulty electric blanket.

So it was with great gratitude that 'Lassie's sign' in the sky was seen.

The following day I visited an elderly lady and told her the story of Lassie as she was always interested in such things. Matters of the occult I almost said, but it is strange that many are afraid of the word occult - its true definition is 'hidden wisdom' - 'esoteric knowledge'. We are instructed to 'seek and ye shall find'. The lady was indeed interested and told me that she had known a lady in Saltash who also had a collie called Lassie. Her Lassie had died one day and that night as she looked out of her door, overhead shot a beautiful shooting star and she automatically called out "There goes my Lassie!"

A few days later I found that Lassie's owner had been known as the Wise Old Woman of Saltash and had been in communication with Winston Churchill during the war.

Charlie

A black and white stray cat, paralysed in his hind limbs, had been brought to me in 1971. He had lain by the side of a house in Saltash when a friendly soul picked him up, knocked on the door of the house and explained about the cat. She was told "Well, he's not ours - he's been lying there for three days and we don't want him!"

The lady took him home and cared for him but she was unable to afford veterinary help for him, though he was in great pain when moved, and only able to pull himself along with his front legs. She was also unable to keep him, living in a council flat and being a widow.

After ten days in her care, the lady brought the sad cat to me for help. On going to lift him from the basket, healing poured into him through my hands, which I then gently rested on his back, asking for help. After several minutes he gazed intently into my eyes and then leapt up onto the windowsill, purring! The 'Good Samaritan' nearly fainted with shock saying, "But he can't do that he's paralysed!" She was absolutely astonished.

We were packed with animals and birds at that time and Dennis was not amused to find yet another joining the family, but all advertisements for Charlie's owner or a new home proved fruitless. We were living hand-to-mouth as it was. All those years ago at the 'Mousehole Wild Birds Hospital' when I wished for my own animal and bird sanctuary, it never occurred to me to also ask for the funds to run it, and the space to accommodate the residents! No one had told me one had to tie up such little loose ends as that!

When we had Charlie neutered, the vet estimated he was some four years old. He remained with us for the next sixteen years of his Earthly life, and during the whole of those years he was my beloved friend and companion, often sitting with that same look of intent into my eyes, seeking to share with me some inner knowledge and understanding of which I was not aware. He appeared on BBC TV 'Nationwide' in 1976, on the healing of birds and animals here, in the small sanctuary of those days.

As the years came and went, I became more aware of spiritual matters and to atonement within, as far as possible, to that greater Something within each and every one of us, and found my awareness gently changing, as the understanding

deepened. In October 1987, my dear friend suddenly lost his sight; at the same time he became totally deaf. He still showed his love by purring happily in one's presence, finding his way onto a lap or into a bed at night, where he found comfort in closeness. He then lost his appetite completely and became

very weak. He was now about twenty years of age.

On the 2nd November, our friend Christine called to see us. She is able, at times, to see radiant Beings of Light, visions, and receive telepathic messages, as I have been privileged to receive on very rare occasions. On this day, a Light Being appeared to Christine giving his name as Markos and informing us that he was Charlie's 'guardian'; that Charlie had come to individuals for eons of time, down through the ages, to help them in their spiritual advancement and in their daily lives; that when his task was again finished, he would return to Markos again, in the Light. The Being explained that I was not to worry about Charlie's condition - just to care for him whilst he was with Frederick and I here at Shalom Ubracha (which means Peace with Blessings). This message helped greatly.

Sadly, the dear lad became thinner and weaker until, after agonizing for two days and nights, we decided to call our kindly vet to come to put him to 'sleep'.

Whilst awaiting the vet, I was impressed to sit down with Charlie, close my eyes and open, at random, *"A Course in Miracles"* (Dr.Helen Schucman), which I had by then been studying deeply for the past three years. Closing my eyes and with Charlie purring contentedly on my lap, I opened the book at the passage "I am as God created me."

Immediately wishing to include my little friend, I changed this, mentally and aloud to "we are as God created us, Charlie! Not the body which I now see you in - and we shall meet again, Charlie, in our Real Selves - in our Real Home!"

Peace came as we waited for the vet to call...

At noon that day, Tuesday 17th November, my beloved friend slipped gently and quietly out of his physical garment. All that day I had to keep reminding myself "We are as God created us, Charlie we are Spirit and you are not dead, but alive, somewhere, be happy; see you!"

The following morning, I was suddenly overcome with the utmost anguish at the physical loss of my old and dear friend - where was he now God?

At that moment Frederick called to me that Christine was on the telephone. I walked sadly down the stairs. She was agog with excitement! After taking her young son to school, the steering wheel of her car refused to turn into her driveway - instead, her car took her down to her nearby beach car park, where she then sat, wondering what on earth it was all about and not knowing that Charlie was 'dead'.

Quite suddenly a message was channelled through, very quickly and very clearly. Fortunately pen and paper were close to hand and as fast as her hand could write, the words poured through - from Charlie!

"My time has come to leave you.
I have returned to my Light Source
Do not grieve over my suffering
I have journeyed many times and can rise above my body.
My Light Source is always waiting.
You are following the right path, Marilyn -
My love and light shine upon you and Frederick.
Do not forget - I am still only a whisper away!"

What a tremendously uplifting message from our 'little' friend! What a marvellous answer to a prayer! A miracle! It turned my sorrow into great joy for him, and though I still miss his physical presence, I try to keep in mind his words and to more fully understand and realise them in their Reality.

A few days later a friend asked how Charlie was. I explained that he had 'passed on' at noon on the Tuesday.

"But he can't have. I passed your house at four o'clock on Tuesday, on my way to the post box, and he was playing in your garden, leaping around like a youngster. If there had been time I was going to call in and ask what miracle cure you had given him in his old age! I called him and he came over to 'speak' to me, then went back to playing again. It was lovely to see him looking so young and active once more!"

I asked if she was quite sure it was Charlie.

"Oh yes I know Charlie as well as I know my own cat, Marilyn!"

Charlie had worn a cat's body in this incarnation, but who is he in Reality? What great souls inhabit animal or bird bodies in this third dimensional world of ours, which we only see with our very limited physical sight? What great missions are some of the Animal Kingdom on and do we help or hinder them in their tasks, in their own as well as in our evolutions? How dreadfully sad for those unfortunate creatures imprisoned in factory farms, research laboratories, zoos and such. What a dreadful karmic debt we shall have to pay, to these Creatures of God...We are asked to "Do unto others as you would be done by." Perhaps we should really try to do just that?

Bumble's Miracle

Some years ago a friend brought a lady on holiday from Hampshire to see our birds and animals, especially the blind squirrel, Fliptod, who lived in our Linden tree in the garden. Judith was very interested in stories of their various healings.

Late one night in mid-November of that year, Judith telephoned me from Hampshire. A friend of hers was in a desperate state for her beloved cat Bumble who was dying of cancer. Could we pray and ask for healing help for him please, and his owner Valerie?

Saying that of course we would, but could promise nothing, that we would mentally ask for healing help for Bumble and also his desperate owner, Judith replied that she would ring her friend right away to tell her.

I have to say here that at the time I was terribly depressed, something that has dogged me practically all my life, at times, unfortunately and really felt I could do nothing at all to help Bumble or his owner. Having put the telephone down I looked at the wall in the study and said through my tears of despair "Well Lord, there's nothing I can do to help but if you're listening can you help this poor cat and his owner, please?" My heart went out to them both but I really felt there was no hope, when one is down everything seems hopeless!

Two days later Judith telephoned again to say "Thank you for Bumble's healing, Valerie is writing…"

Another two days later, we received the following letter, which I shall always keep. It was the most poignant and beautifully hand-written letter I think I have had the privilege to receive -

Dear Marilyn Preston

As I sit here tonight, looking at my beautiful, bouncing cat Bumble, I can hardly believe that a week ago I was filled with desolation and hopelessness.

But first may I introduce myself? My name is Valerie Miles and one of my closest friends is Judith who 'phoned you to tell you about our poor sick cat. Judith had spoken to me some weeks ago when she returned from her holiday in your area and had related many wonderful tales of healing. An animal lover myself I, of course, was thrilled and fascinated with her accounts.

This time last week my little Bumble was dying. He had taken no food or drink since the previous Friday. The vet told us that our beautiful cat was dehydrated and took a blood sample which, we learned the next day showed the dreaded leukaemia together with some kidney damage caused by the disease. We were told that there was very little that could be done and our anguish knew no bounds.

In distress I spoke to Judith who suggested 'phoning to tell you about it, after which she rang to let me know what you had said. I cannot tell you the inexpressible comfort I found in just knowing that you had heard about it - I could not explain or understand it, but something intangible had reached out and touched me and my grief lessened to some measure.

Late last Tuesday night I told Bumble that you were praying for him and that help was on its way. For five days he had been almost motionless, prostrate on the floor, no twitch of the ear nor flicker of the eye just wasting away. Early on Wednesday morning I repeated it to him over and over again.

Then I saw a miracle happen. My little Bumble purred and stood up and rubbed against me - but how can I describe a miracle? It was emotion and spirit and wonder rolled into one and I knew at that moment that something marvellous had taken place and that I had been truly privileged to see it. I cried and hugged him and offered thanks to God.. and I feel very humble.

The vet is amazed....

I wish I could find words to express all my feelings but in fact there are no words to express them. How can I give thanks? What can I say? How could I tell you how much my spirit has been restored? When I see around me so much to fill me with despair, there is a message from God full of hope and joy to lift me high and wing me to a much finer spiritual awareness.

As Bumble continues to make good progress, how wide the ripple flows. Many people close to me have been touched by a keener perception of spiritual thought. How good to have seen the power of prayer manifesting itself in a little cat. How great is the work of God.

Although I am unknown to you, you have given me something rare - the gift of faith - and in this I have been given all the gifts of the world. My cup runneth over.
With my thanks and love
Valerie Miles.

That Christmas we received a photograph of Bumble, just taken - a very happy cat, totally healed and once more whole. We could do nothing but 'Someone up There' had heard and most kindly did! The next Christmas another lovely photo of the handsome Bumble arrived, pondering in his garden *'Sometimes I sits and thinks and sometimes I just sits.'*
Perhaps he understood more than we do.

It may be of comfort to know that we are perhaps not so alone as we often think we are and that we can mentally ask for help on the long way Home.

Valerie and I kept in touch over the years but in 1987 she telephoned and said she had been diagnosed with cancer herself and was already having treatment. I wrote to her on the 15th December a lengthy letter, telling her about the passing of my beloved cat Charlie and his 'return' and message.

On the 24th December I received a letter from her husband with the very sad news that *"My dear Valerie commenced the next great journey at eight o'clock last Sunday evening 20th December. I was with her up to the end of her*

117

time in this world. She is the love of my life and I have a mountain of memories to carry me through once this immediate sadness has been eased by the magic of time. I thank you and Frederick for all the comfort you brought to her and of course I and Valerie are eternally grateful to you for keeping Bumble with us. He is slumbering on the chair close to me now.

Valerie wrote out the following pieces from the Bible to be read at her funeral: Ecclesiastes Ch.3 vs 1-9 and Isiah Ch.40 vs 28-31……. Bless you both……."

Valerie had become very weak, with the condition and the aggressive treatment towards the end, and was very weary. Looking up the Isaiah quotation I was deeply moved with the words "But they that wait upon the Lord shall renew their strength, they shall mount up with the wings as eagles, they shall run, and not be weary and they shall walk and not faint."

In a long letter from Valerie's husband in 1995, after Bumble's passing, it includes *" I can never replace Bumble.. he was unique, he would fall asleep in the garden and birds would feed around him, he never chased anything except the breeze-blown tops of Dandelions and never harmed even the noisiest of bluebottles. He would leap from the top of the fridge onto my shoulders and wrap himself around them like a mohair scarf - with warm, deep purrs that made sweeter music than any Pavarotti!*

"Oft do I think of him; there are times when I am in the kitchen here and something makes me glance to the back door window pane and for a second I see him sitting on the window sill leaning forward to peep into the backdoor glass. Nodding his head of old saying 'yes I want to come in now'. So real I could touch him - and then he is gone back to his playground in the warm meadow of eternal summer and a never ending supply of dandelion blooms.

"In 1981, when Valerie told me she had got in touch with you I did not really believe anything would come of it, but I did witness the sad state of him and he was off his legs and lying down and truly dying. When I came home that day and he was walking around, Valerie was over the moon with joy. It will always be one of the greatest moments in my whole life…

118

"I hope to write to you again if you are not bored by my ramblings. Stay well, Marilyn, and you, Frederick, all good wishes and blessings to you...."

Simon, the Irish Red Setter

One of the many healing stories in Rebecca Hall's book *'Animals are Equal'* was about Simon who was suffering badly for many months with serious gastric troubles, his owner Jean Cook wrote to Rebecca. She explained the vet was very sympathetic to healing, told her she had a very sick dog, that he had severe internal inflammation. But no amount of pills and injections could cure him. Jean and her husband Derek brought Simon for healing for three weeks running and thankfully Simon was healed and became his lovely happy self once more, living for several years with them and their three cats.

However, then we learned that Jean had cancer very badly and was not expected to live. Derek telephoned one evening in great distress. Simon was now old and very ill and they had arranged for the vet to call in a few minutes time and he was very concerned about the terrible effect it was going to have on Jean as she was in such despair. Would I please send out thoughts for Jean and Simon?

Very choked with this sad news I said of course I would do that and hoped that Simon would have a quick release from his now worn out body and head straight for the Light and his great new freedom. Also that Jean would feel only relief for her wonderful and devoted friend and would not suffer the grief expected, that Derek too would be spared the anguish of the parting of his beloved dog.

Putting the phone down I was immediately swamped with the most indescribable grief and felt my heart would literally break. It was as though I was going through appalling anguish which knew no bounds and sobbed for hours until I went to sleep absolutely drained and worn out with no more tears left to cry. Nothing could console the deep pain and loss I felt.

The next morning Derek rang and thanked me 'for whatever it is you did!' Both he and Jean had felt no grief at the parting with Simon and he was absolutely amazed that she had taken it so well, just feeling relief that Simon's suffering was over and that he was at peace. I couldn't tell Derek that I had obviously taken on all their combined anguish and had gone through hell. I hope I don't have to do that again and have no idea why it happened as they were not particularly close friends and we had not seen them all for years. It's not all happiness and miracles being a healer.

Some of the other letters Rebecca received from relieved pet owners for her book include the story of Topsy, a black and white farm cat who was apparently tossed by a cow, whose horn went through her lower jaw and tongue. Topsy's jaw was wired by a vet but she was unable to eat or drink anything for a week. Her owner asked for absent healing for the cat and next morning Topsy was looking for her food and water. Three days later, the letter said, it was hard to tell anything had happened to her.

Around the same time, four more cats' owners requested absent healing - all for their cats whose jaws were broken - never before nor since has such a request been asked. I did 'mental' operations on each of these cats and within hours they were eating and drinking normally again.

The story is told too of a boxer dog who had cancer of the lymph glands and recovered after contact healing, only to succumb again and involving his kidneys. Healing was given and also the Dr. Edward Bach Flower Remedies (and to the

121

owner who was worried out of her mind) and thankfully both recovered very well.

Another Boxer was brought from Newton Abbot in Devon with gangrene in his foreleg, with the bone visible - a very nasty condition indeed. The smell from the gangrene was appalling, but putting my hand over it and silently asking for help Leo was good as gold and stayed quietly looking into my eyes whilst I mentally told him that all possible help was being given from 'Upstairs' and we hoped he'd be fine soon. I was delighted to hear that three days later no-one could even see where the condition had been. How can I not believe in miracles?

Another Simon in *'Animals are Equal'* was a beagle owned by Ann and Edward Smail of Burgess Hill in Sussex. They wrote to Rebecca that Simon was injured at nine and a half years of age - he began to limp and was later chased by a workman when they heard him scream. They immediately took him to a vet who diagnosed the first injury as a partly damaged tendon in his back right leg and the second as having severed it. For the best part of a year the vet did all he could but Simon limped badly and then his hip started to waste away. The vets decided to cut out the knee joint and pack it with only a fifty fifty chance of any success. Mrs Smail wrote to me on the Thursday explaining the operation to take place the following Monday. I immediately wrote back on receipt of the letter on the Saturday and said I would try a mental operation on Simon.

On the Sunday Edward Smail took Simon out for his 'daily hobble' as they put it in their letter and returned shortly afterwards absolutely astounded. Their dog was walking normally and had not limped since. Four months later they had to see their vet as Simon had an inflamed eye and he too was astounded to see Simon was fine, saying 'Quite right too. More and more vets and doctors are going to healers for that extra bit of help they cannot give themselves'.

Years later Simon developed a bad kidney infection and they feared it was the end but thankfully he again responded beautifully to absent healing and when his owners wrote to Rebecca he was then a healthy fifteen year old.

Then there was Donnie a lovely German Shepherd, only nine months old, who was brought in one Monday evening and due to be put down on Wednesday because of a collapsed pancreas. Vets had done all they could. Mr Dickinson brought him over from Plymouth, extremely thin and weak and hardly able to stand as he had had to be on a very meagre diet. I felt there was really nothing to lose for the dear lad and suggested they give him what he wanted to eat. The owners brought Donnie for healing once a week for five weeks and Mr Dickinson wrote to Rebecca *"from the day we took him to Marilyn he hasn't taken any form of tablet. He has put on over two stone and his coat looks really healthy. My opinion is that without Marilyn's help and love for animals we would not have got very far. I have no doubt in my mind about healers and would advise to trust them and believe that they can do some marvellous things."*

As I have explained elsewhere I really don't understand how these miracles happen - "Of myself I can do nothing - it is the Father within who doeth the works" I often 'look up' (or rather within) and say "How on earth did You do that then?"

Then we come to Peggy and Drummon Chapman from Kent who wrote and asked for absent healing for their yellow Labrador Sheba, crippled with arthritis for years at only four and a half years old, also for their Beagle Louise, in agony with a slipped disc in her shoulder for a month. Louise had immediate improvement and total healing in two weeks. Sheba, hardly able to walk by now took a little longer, with "complete relief in eight to ten weeks" they wrote.

Ben and Morti

Hazel contacted me one day from Looe in Cornwall. She heard I gave healing and one of her cats had cancer. Ben had been a stray and it took her several weeks before she could coax the cat to her for food - he would only eat it if it was left somewhere for him to get at. He always looked poorly and ill.

Eventually Ben was cajoled into coming into the house and gradually became part of the family, with Hazel, Derek and their other rescued cats. He was then taken to the vet's and 'seen to' with a good checking over - but the prognosis was not good. His coat was long and meant to be black, but did not quite make it - it was all over the show and they, secretly out of his earshot, called him the 'coconut mat cat'. But Ben's character was lovely - and that was the main thing.

He teamed up with Mortimore, and he and Morti became great pals. Hazel would often take Ben to the vet's and come on to see me, so Ben could have some contact healing to top him up. We all enjoyed the sessions and he could not have found a better home in Cornwall. He was greatly loved.

One day the telephone rang and it was Hazel in tears. Ben had just died, then we were both in tears and neither could speak much. I said how terribly sorry I was and could share the grief at this sad loss. But Ben had known human love, kindness and companionship, perhaps for the first time in his life and I hoped that he would have a safe and happy journey now to his 'real' Home. I also explained to Hazel that he could come back and tell them he was okay and doing fine, if so would she please let me know.

That very evening she rang to say that her husband had called her from another room, excitedly saying that he had just seen Ben on the mantelpiece! Smiling! Hazel entered the room, there was no sign of Ben "You must be seeing things Derek, what on earth are you talking about, Ben wouldn't be the mantelpiece he died this morning"

Derek replied "I know it sounds ridiculous, but I'm an accountant and I have to account for everything. I **saw** Ben on the mantelpiece, but can't account for it".

Obviously Hazel could not accept that Derek had seen Ben. Why was he smiling? Well, he couldn't stand heights before, so perhaps that's why he's very pleased not to be afraid of heights now!

Christmas came and went and Hazel used up the film she had in her camera but leaving it in there, including a shot of Ben before he died.

Months later, one morning came an urgent call from Hazel. Could she please come and see me?

"Yes of course - I've no appointments this morning, do you want to come now?"

Shesaid she had something amazing to show me.

When she came to the front door Hazel was looking quite puzzled and worried. Ten days after Ben had died and been buried, Morti was lying out in the sunshine in their lounge and looked so lovely that she felt she would like to take a photo of him. Getting the camera she found the last picture had been taken and the film used up so removed it for processing later. She put a new film in and hurried back into the lounge to take the shot of Morti before he moved or woke up. But looking at him through the view finder she found she was looking at **Ben**. Thinking she was going mad she moved the camera and still found she was looking at the 'coconut mat cat' not the shiny, sleek, black, short haired, sturdy Morti, who looked totally different from Ben of course. She focused on the cat again, it was still Ben, lying perfectly happy on his side, with his claws extending and retracting in great pleasure! Thinking she was by now seeing something totally impossible Hazel took the photo, put the camera aside again and found she was looking at Morti lying on his side, perfectly relaxed in the sunshine. Later she used up the rest of that new film, occasionally wondering what had happened to her mind that day she 'thought 'she saw Ben again.

This morning she had just picked up the film from the developers and brought the photos for me to see. The first picture is of BEN lying stretched out in the sunshine on his side in their lounge, with claws outstretched in his ecstacy - unmistakeably the lovable long-haired, browny-black, coconut mat cat - the image of a photo taken of him before he 'died', in the previous film taken months

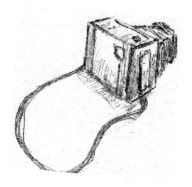

before. It was obviously not coincidental that Hazel had had to put a new film in the camera on that sunny morning to take a photo of Morti in her lounge - and here was beloved Ben, the first picture in the new film, large as life and proving it!

Knowing that Morti and Ben were close companions it is my thought that Morti agreed to allow Ben to 'take over' his body for that one photo to convince his still grieving Mum that he was indeed fine, well and happy! Well done Morti and Ben! It is good to look at the treasured photos here on my desk as I write this, two of Morti (with his friend Tuppy), sitting up, bright eyed and bushy tailed as they say, and two of Ben - one before and one after 'death' but unmistakably Ben. They say the camera doesn't lie and in this case we are quite sure it didn't.

Peterkins, Whisky & Sandy

A friend had been telling me about her animal companions who had each meant so much to her in life. Peter (alias Peterkins or Sausage) one day jumped into a Fyffes banana lorry which had called in at her father's nursery in Cobham, Surrey. The curious cat inspected the lorry with interest. Later, Peter was nowhere to be found by Joyce and her parents.

Then they had a telephone call from the lorry driver at his base twelve miles away at Kingston-upon Thames, explaining that a cat had jumped out of the back of the lorry and scurried away, and that he had remembered the cat as being theirs.

Joyce was desperate and her father took her backwards and forwards on the main London to Portsmouth road, but there was no sign of beloved Sausage.

Six weeks of worry went by. Then one night, Joyce heard scratching at her bedroom door (they lived in a bungalow and there were long glass doors as well as a single window in her bedroom); it was night time and Joyce called to her parents who immediately came to investigate and there was the most bedraggled Peterkins you could ever imagine. His coat was wet and torn, an eye bleeding, his paws all bleeding, thoroughly worn out, underfed and completely exhausted.

They all greeted him with such affection and tears, relief and joy. Out came a tin of best salmon which he hungrily devoured and then slept for the next forty-eight hours. Never did he investigate visiting lorries or cars after that episode!

But he continued his routine of scampering through adjoining woodland to come up to the Portsmouth road to meet Joyce as she got off the bus at six thirty each evening. He never walked down the lane with her but continued in the woods alongside. When Joyce reached the nursery gates, Peterkins would jump out on her and they always treated this as a surprise and a joke. Without fail, wind, sun or snow, he would be there.

When Joyce was hospitalised for three weeks, Joyce's mother later told her that he still made the journey to the bus stop every evening and would return without her, totally dejected.

Sometime in the sixties, the family moved to Saltash. Joyce and her parents travelled down from Surrey to Saltash in her little mini with their tranquillised cat Binky and Whisky the mongrel taking up the remaining room in the car.

Binky and Whisky quickly adapted to their new surroundings and each evening Joyce's father would walk round the block with Whisky, Binky the cat always trailing a few yards behind.

In 1969 Joyce's father suddenly died, leaving much sadness. Whisky used to sit outside their gate looking, watching, waiting for his master who never appeared, shedding real tears when Joyce's mother talked to him saying that she missed him deeply too.

Wibin two weeks Whisky died and Binky followed just three days after; their little graves and headstones with shrubs around them are all that seems to be left of them…yet they live on, as we all shall, and one fine day…..

But now we come to another little friend, Sandy, a lovely ginger cat with an immaculate white bib. I think it was round about Christmas 1986 when Sandy became very ill; he was getting on in years but something was very wrong. The vet examined him gently and realised that Sandy's kidneys had just about ceased functioning and had 'powdered' as he put it. Nevertheless he did everything possible to seek to help the stricken cat, also using homeopathic remedies.

On the 19th February I was invited to give the sad cat some healing. Sandy and I enjoyed our healing sessions together, twice a week, and soon he was able to get up and down the stairs more ably, jump on his favourite chair and the bed, once more. He was still 'not right' by a long way, but at least he seemed to enjoy life quite a bit more again, and at times would play with the strings on my anorak, or with a twig in the garden when we took our walk down there before or after the healing time.

Sandy would normally greet me and when we rubbed noses his purr would warm my heart. Then he would turn his back to me, whilst sitting comfortably on the floor, lie down, and wait for my hands to be placed gently over his kidney area, soaking in the warmth of the treatment.

Joyce and I would leave notes for each other on his progression, as I would call on the mornings she had to work, so that he was not alone for long periods of time. It was lovely to read, for instance: "I really feel he has turned a corner. He seems brighter, still eating little, but content to return to some of his former routines, which perhaps indicates a greater degree of security...."

And so our meetings continued, with the hope that Sandy would be able to fully respond and live happily with Tom and Joyce for a few more companionable years.

One day a telephone call from Joyce said that Tom had rescued a fledgling blackbird from a neighbour's cat the previous evening, kept it overnight, then put it by a bush in the morning as the parents were back looking for their missing youngster. A little later Sandy raced down the stairs and waited impatiently at the back door to be allowed out. Joyce opened the door and Sandy shot out, presumably in a rush to spend a penny.

Sandy did not usually spend much time on his own in the garden as he was terrified of two other cats. Noticing that he was taking rather a long time about it, Joyce went out to look for him. To her horror, she saw Sandy sitting in the middle of the lawn with the baby blackbird between his front legs. However, on the point of running down into the garden to rescue the little bird from him, she saw a most extraordinary thing. Suddenly, from one side of the garden one of the other cats came hurrying stealthily to get the quarry he had lost the previous evening.

For the first time, Sandy stood his ground and instead of running away as he usually did, spat at the intruder in his garden, with the young bird safely nesting in his chest. From the other side, then came the second cat to get the bird. Again our hero spat and lashed out with his claws this time, showing them both he was not prepared to relinquish his guardianship.

With a great sigh of relief (and pride at this wonderful attitude of her much beloved cat), Joyce hurried into the garden, gently picked up the little blackbird and put him into the greenhouse with some food and fresh water. She then telephoned me to see what could be done, whilst Sandy stood guard outside the greenhouse door, until I went over to collect the fledgling. Sandy had done a marvellous job and his Mum and Dad were delighted, as indeed we were to see this side of his protective nature appearing.

Unfortunately, two mornings later, our little fledgling patient was dead. His physical body was, rather. He was such a good fellow, taking food and drink readily and being quite perky and bright, hence it was quite a shock to find he did not make it here, in his present incarnation. But, of course he lives on, and perhaps...

Back to Sandy. I continued to pop over to see him and give healing a couple of times a week and he had his ups and downs. Meanwhile our friends badly needed a holiday and we were taking over the care of Sandy until their return.

However, on the Saturday night before they were due to leave Sandy became extremely ill. Joyce and Tom were up all night with him and in the end came to the decision that it would be kinder, at last, to have the vet put him gently to sleep next day, for apart from this latest illness, he had been off his food for a long time, despite every dish imaginable to be tempted with. They were also very concerned at having to leave their little friend, especially if he had become desperately ill whilst they were away for a week, leaving us with the responsibility of what then to do; if it had to be , they would have wished to be there 'at the end' so that he did not feel deserted.

Their holiday had been all arranged and they both desperately needed a break. To anyone who loves animals, it will be obvious how very torn they both felt.

About eleven thirty on the Sunday morning, a tearful voice on the telephone said: "Marilyn, we have had to make an awfully difficult and hard decision. Would you like to come over and say goodbye to our dear Sandy, please?"

Joyce and I were both in tears as we met. Tom had discreetly 'disappeared' for the time. Sad at heart, we went into the lounge. Sandy got up to greet us, then smiled and began purring turning round, as he always did, and lying on the floor with his back to me so that my hands could be placed over his back and kidneys. Rays of the morning sun lit up his golden ginger coat, now looking a little worse for wear and illness. He totally relaxed and continued gently purring. Suddenly Joyce and I felt much better too. The decision made felt 'right', and our hearts were lifted again, and we felt that Sandy was quite happy with the decision about his future. "Thank you I can cope alright now Marilyn".

The veterinary surgeon was due at noon, to slip a needle quite painlessly into Sandy, to release him to his new life. He had had some very bad bouts of sickness and suffering at times and one is often torn between whether to continue to try and overcome certain conditions or to say it's time…it is not easy to say goodbye to a companion of fifteen years. The mental agony one experiences is often of deep anguish and I knew this to be true of Joyce and possibly with her husband also: they had both been kindness itself to me throughout Sandy's illness, and much appreciated any help given with the healing. "You know how much we appreciate your kindness and dedication to Sandy. This morning you imparted the confidence and courage his illness had deprived him of. He is happy and comfortable now…"

Our prayer for him then, at the farewell, had been that he will be released into God's care, that he will find all that his Soul longs for, that he will find peace and happiness, perhaps be able to impress his loved ones left behind that that is indeed so, for no matter how hard one tries, the grief at the loss of a loved one is very often hard to bear. It leaves a large gap in our lives, an empty space, a silence impossible to ignore, an aching heart, a deep grief within. Until we can see it in a different light, that is.

The following day, Tom went down into the garden early, but before he got there, he was startled to see Sandy sitting on the wall, in another favourite spot of his, looking down into the beautiful garden. Tom blinked and looked again

131

and there was Sandy, looking marvellous as he turned his head to look at Tom, mouth curved upwards in his smile, eyes happy, yet serene. Standing still, Tom deliberately blinked again and Sandy had 'gone'.

Thoughtfully, Tom made his way upstairs to tell Joyce of his encounter; she then explained to him that precisely the same thing had happened the day before, shortly after their Sandy had been 'put to sleep', when she saw him at the top of their garden path.

The next day was Tuesday and the first day of their much needed holiday. I was to go in twice a day to bring in the post which often used to get caught up in the letter box and being local election time also, many items were being dropped through, or jamming up, before dropping into the television room. Noticing that the door of the room was left ajar, about eightinches, I immediately thought "Ah, yes that's been left open for Sandy to go in and out and jump onto 'his' settee when he wants to." Hence, I was most careful every time I went into the room, twice daily, to collect the mail, election notices, papers, circulars and such like to leave the door in that exact position.

On the Friday morning, I went into the house, through the kitchen and the dining room, out into the hall and stood stock still in terror. The television room door was wide open!

As soon as I could move, I fled through the house and stood, shaking like a leaf outside the back door. Someone had broken in! He was probably hiding behind a door ready to knock me over the head! Perhaps he'd already rifled the house and left! My mind ran riot over what 'he' could have done - or would do!

I had to literally force myself to go into the house again, get to the television room, pick up the several items posted through the letter box and make a hasty retreat out and then home again. A dose of Dr. Edward Bach's Rescue Remedy was called for and I took this with chattering teeth and lips.

Should I phone the police? How on earth would I explain I knew I had left the television room door open because it was for a 'dead' cat to walk through! (Anyway, they walk through doors, walls and whatever when we see them, as this plane is only 'solid' in appearance to us still here living on it.) I couldn't tell the neighbours as they would be too frightened of burglars on the prowl. In great worry I waited until Frederick came home from work and we went over to check everything was alright, which it was, thankfully. We agreed it would not be wise to tell Tom and Joyce as it would worry them too much. But how had the door come to be wide open?

Frederick was able to accompany me for the next few days. Then it was homecoming for our friends as the Tuesday had come around again. We spoke with them on the telephone early that evening.

Next morning we had a note popped through the door. *"Did you have faulty electric last night? Everything flickered for two hours here, in all the rooms. We wondered! Used to get the 'cold' treatment on return from holidays from our Sandy - real anger that he had been left! Interesting quickie - latterly I used to sneeze when Sandy came onto the bed at night - sometimes up to ten times. I did this three times, on alternate nights on holiday, on getting into bed. Even Tom remarked on this 'coincidence'. We dreaded coming into the house yesterday...The flowers were a lovely welcoming surprise - thank you for everything. See you soon."*

When we met there was much to talk about. And the electricity - no, we'd had no problem with the lights on Tuesday night between nine and eleven - nor had any other neighbours to our knowledge. They wondered if it was Sandy showing his disapproval of them leaving him. Yet by the sneezing on alternate nights, it appeared he may well have joined them on their holiday on at least three occasions!

Then I mentioned about the inner door being wide open and frightening me out of my wits and it suddenly struck us that there again Sandy could have possibly achieved this, too, as well as using his powers to interfere with the electricity for two hours.

A short while later the telephone rang. It was Joyce. Just before we had spoken earlier, she had made their bed, smoothing out everything as always, including the counterpane on the top, perfectly, without a crease or wrinkle, the bed which Sandy so used to love to jump up onto, on 'his' bottom corner of it.

After our talk, she had gone upstairs to the bedroom for something and there, facing her, was the firm impression made in the counterpane of where a certain puss called Sandy had quite obviously just lain! He obviously was where he wanted to be!

And on Sunday 23rd August, Joyce was with her mother in their garden, when she was able to see their beloved little friend once more, this time walking across to the bottom of the garden.

Many people are privileged to see their loved ones after apparent death, and I am sure the day will come when the veils will thin between the different dimensions so that it will become the accepted norm, and so will begin the new awaking, or rather re-awakening of Spirit Truths, for we are all spirit, encompassed by a temporary physical form, the spirit is of the real world, the form of this world only. The likeness of God which we are made of, is the SPIRIT - of everyone and everything - we are all of God, all God's children, there are no distinctions in God's Mind.

Very often when sitting or lying on the floor giving Sandy healing, I would talk to him about life continuing, that whatever happened he would not die only leave his 'overcoat' behind like a butterfly leaving its cocoon behind after its miraculous transformation from a totally different looking being, a caterpillar- and that, for some reason, as yet unknown to us, he had become ill, but we were trying to get him feeling better and 'right' again; that in Reality in our REAL SELVES, we are whole, perfect and happy; that somehow we have got our physical selves and minds in a bit of a tangle, 'down here'. During these talks with Sandy he would often turn his head to look into my eyes to seek the truth of what I was trying to explain to him, and he would know, gently half-closing his eyes and bursting into a new bout of purring, deeply content for a while.

Just after noon on Sunday 31st May 1987, when Sandy departed this dimension we were all thinking about him, of course, and wishing him well. Would his young blackbird friend be there to greet him?

At about one thirty during lunch with her husband and mother, however, Joyce was suddenly startled to see a figure outside the patio doors of their dining room - the figure of Sandy! He was sitting just outside at the top of the path, looking down into the garden, a favourite spot of his. She deliberately blinked and looked again and there he was, large as life and looking very beautiful. She mentally spoke to him and he turned his head to look at her, his mouth curved up in his pleased expression, his eyes happy, his coat in its perfection. She blinked again and he was gone.

Joyce had felt it unwise to mention the fact to her husband or her mother, who came each Sunday to spend the day with them, but in a lovely card slipped through our door that day, after telephoning me about Sandy's return, she wrote *"Marilyn, the rest you know, after Sandy's considerable suffering over the past twenty four hours. I tried to write calmly and factually, but you know my hidden feelings. That little soul left with so much love and gave us so much. That look at the top of the path told me of his relief and happiness, and it was a proud and confident Sandy who smiled at me...."*

Dorial
by
Gaynor M Hunt

Whenever I read the poem "Banshee" by Will H Ogilvie my heart swells in recollection of the magnificent stallion 'Dorial' and how he was healed through the gifts of Marilyn Preston Evans.

In the spring of 1987 I'd advertised for an Arab stallion to loan as a husband for my mares. Amongst the many potential suitors, Dorial's name appeared. My research revealed he had been bred at one of the top studs in England and that his bloodlines were second to none. So his name headed the list of stallions to view.

His owner was very ill in hospital and unable to look after him. So a 'committee' of three female friends had been formed to attend to Dorial. When I went to see him I discovered he hadn't been out of his stable for three months! I was told he had a problem with doorways and would rush through in a panic, so they wouldn't take him out to show him to me. His owner must have been able to handle him but I could see that these ladies found it easier to keep him inside.

Obviously I had to get him out and give him some exercise and to see him properly. Well, I only wish someone had had a camera on them that day! He came out of his stable at 100mph and was rearing and plunging all over the place. I managed to lead him across a field and the 'committee' watched as I lunged him for thirty minutes. After only a short while I could see how much he appreciated being able to stretch his legs and enjoy himself. More to the point, I knew my search was over and that I had to take him on. He was so beautiful I'd lost my heart to him.

I went back again a few days later and repeated what I'd done, much to the 'committee's' relief. The day came to collect Dorial and this led to the first of many injuries from him, a kick to the knee. This rather took the stuffing out of me as it came out of the blue. Perhaps if I'd known what lay ahead

I would have left him behind then and there. But I was thrilled with the prospect of having foals from him.

Now I had kept stallions before, I respected and loved them. I thought that Dorial would respond to kind words, gentle handling and a different lifestyle, but it made no difference. Even allowing for him settling into his new home, where he could go out every day, he was problematical. His barging through any door or gateway was a serious habit, which at eighteen years of age, he'd become used to. I couldn't find out why he did it, I assumed he'd had a fright once and got jammed, but I wanted to help him overcome the fixation.

He kicked holes in the stable walls, bared his teeth and used them to great effect whenever he could. No one but myself could safely walk past his door without him racing over with his ears back, teeth at the ready! When he bit, he ran

to the back of his box, trembling, waiting for the severe reprimand. I had to carry a stick for my own protection when I was with him, but the situation was making me very unhappy. It was not my way of looking after horses at all.

The dysfunctional behaviour didn't end in his stable. Every day I'd lead him out to his three acre field. And he would spend all his time at the gate. The grass was never eaten! I couldn't understand it. He wouldn't even go off and run, explore and play, he'd just stand there and I would keep popping out to talk to him. He seemed insecure, almost agoraphobic, and he couldn't wait to get back into his stable.

When his owner came out of hospital, I started to ask questions about his past. I knew his owner was devoted to him and had been successful showing him, so what had caused all this? The harsh facts of his earlier life began to emerge.

Sadly, when Dorial left his wonderful birthplace, he went to a very 'competitive' establishment. It was while he was at this stud that his present owner met him, as she worked there. If Dorial didn't win when he went to a show, he was whipped when he got home. The man responsible had a foul temper apparently, but also he was a coward. So Dorial couldn't defend himself while he was being beaten, a dustbin lid was held up to his head.

Suddenly, this explained to me why he would become violent whenever I came to change his hay net. It was because he saw the large round shape looming up, as I hoist it to it's fastening on the wall in his stable! I was always vulnerable doing this job, as it took both hands, and on one occasion, I very nearly lost my left eye as he came at me. I know I could have tied him up, but that just succeeded in making him extremely worried about what we were going to do. What could I do to help him understand he had nothing to fear? How do you undo years of abuse?

The one really enduring thing Dorial used to demonstrate, for his favourite Polo treat, was what I called his 'smile'. He would turn his head and neck over so his nose was at right angles to the ground. Then his lips would be drawn up into a closed smile! No one could resist the pose and he would go to greater and greater extremes if he were ignored. I'd never seen any horse do anything like it before and wondered how he'd been taught this 'trick'. Of course I should have realised, with his history, that he hadn't been coached. It was his owner's belief that, because his stable at that other place was behind outbuildings, and permanently in the dark, Dorial used to crane his head to try and see what little light reached his stable door.

All of this, and more, convinced me that Dorial's problems were all of the mind and emotions and not the body. But back in 1987, where and what help was there for an old 'mad' stallion? I turned to Marilyn, his only hope, could absent healing bring him peace and trust?

Although the healing was sent, Marilyn felt that there was some underlying issue that was not being resolved with Dorial. I started visiting her in the evenings, and the pendulum would come out of its box! Marilyn and I spent so many hours in her kitchen trying to penetrate the deep scars around him. Eventually it was the wonderful affinity Marilyn has for the Dr Bach Flower Remedies that caused a breakthrough.

She found that we could communicate with Dorial's Higher Self, and it came as a shock to me to discover now that he was actually having a nervous breakdown. First, the abuse, and now he was separated from the person who had saved him from that abuse, his owner. He missed her. She had witnessed his plight at that terrible place, and in order to rescue him she had defied everyone's advice and bought him. Such loyalty was a tremendous bond between them.

So, in the first of many bottles of those truly miraculous remedies, Dorial received Cherry Plum, Beech, Wild Oat and willow. Every time a bottle was finished, a fresh consultation with his Higher Self would advise what remedy and the dosage. All this was incredible knowledge to me, but it was working. Endless hours of patient, kind concern from Marilyn, she also visited him, although I daren't tell her what he was capable of, or she may never have entered the stable with him!

Slowly, an improvement became noticeable to others before I recognised it myself. It took many months, but I found I could work with him better. I could at last trust him, and I felt he trusted me too. I knew he would never love me as he did his owner, and that was only right, but he'd come to understand.

When I knew the time was coming for Dorial to leave me, Marilyn had found he required only one remedy, Walnut. A bottle was duly made up for the new people who were to carry on looking after him, as, by now my own health problems meant I couldn't. On the 16th march 1989, the day he was to go, I received a phone call from Marilyn to say Dorial had been in touch, and that he didn't need the Walnut or any of the other flower remedies, anymore. He was going to be OK.

Without Marilyn's devotion and compassion, I don't like to dwell on what might have become of dear Dorial. Horses with mental problems are something conventional medicine has no cure for. He turned out to be one of the greatest teachers I have been privileged to work with, I shall always be so grateful he came into our lives.

Animals in the Afterlife

On the 19th March 1992 our friend Christine came to visit and to receive healing. Quite often during such sessions Christinehas fascinating visions and communications which have been most enlightening. This time I was impressed to ask her if she minded having the tape-recorder in the room in case anything happened and could be recorded. Never before or since have I suggested this.

The instant I switched the tape-recorder on Christin's inner vision switched on and an exact hour's taping was recorded from start to finish which we were delighted to find included the following verbatim, on the animals in the next world (or is it a parallel world?). I hope dear reader you will find it as wonderful as we did and interpret as you may, but the essential sense of it is that there is a wonderful world where animals go and it may seem extraordinary but all living things have a 'note' and the instances described are how it sounds from that dimension. We have shared the tape with many people now who have lost animals and many of these have been greatly helped by listening to the following section:-

Christine sees a Powerful Spirit Presence who she has often seen before, usually with the 'Council of Elders' - this time he was on his own to begin with and he asks us:

"Do you ever see your animal with a far away look in his eyes as if he is looking at you and through you? The animals can be here or there. They can be in this world or the next, but still be seen here by us. Do you ever see your animal get excited whilst asleep? Where do you think they are at that moment in time?"

Christine "Oh my goodness! Charlie is sat beside him and he's reaching down and touching his head and saying *"Look at Charlie here - he was often with us even when he was with you."*

"Oh my goodness! Oh my goodness me! Oh my goodness! Now the Spirit has gone like this (he's wearing a deep blue velvet cape and stretches out his arm). Oh, my God!"

141

"Look at what he has come to - look at where he has chosen to stay"

"And there's just loads and loads of water, the sun is just not like the sun here - it's sort of whiter light and it's reflecting on the water and now Charlie is walking towards it and looking back every so often and smiling. And there's all the other animals. THERE'S DANNY! Oh my goodness! And he's still here!" (Danny was Christine's horse - she's crying now.) "And there's my Mum's tortoise - he was twenty-five when he died and he died years ago! And his head's out and he's nodding it up and down. There are just animals everywhere! It's most peculiar, they're all smiling like you know all of them. I can see an elephant and there's this great expanse of water - they are all around the water. There are trees and grass and flowers. Oh - just a minute - what's that? THE FLOWERS ARE SINGING! And the cat, Charlie is now over, rubbing himself against one of these flowers and it's sort of singing a song, or something melodic is coming from it. And the Spirit's cloak - because he's got his arm like this..." (holding out her arm) "...his cloak is as if there's a breeze and this is just..."(here she became lost for words).

I asked about Linda's cat, Baby Black - "He's been there many, many times, but this time he's chosen to stay there. They have the choice."

"OH LOOK!..." (great excitement again) "...I can see Mabel..." (her duck who was killed by a fox the year before) "...on the water! And there's Donald as well..." (killed before Mabel) "...on the water together!"

"Now the Spirit has moved his hand across and I can see a sort of grassy hill and see children playing there. I can still see all the animals and they're rubbing against each other as they go past and rolling over in the grass and everything's really sort of... The grass is really, really green - a sort of different green from the grass here."

I asked about the flowers.

"The flower that is singing is a brilliant white - the petals area brilliant white. I can see into the Beyond - and this seems to go on forever really. Now, now I can see something different. Now I can see people coming towards the animals and

142

wandering amongst them, like saying 'Hello' and talking to them. Now I'm being told that some of these people are here in a dream state..." (whilst asleep at night and out of the physical body) "... and some of these are here - really here. It seems as if you can visit this place in your dreams but it won't feel real, but it is. It's no particular person's job to look after these animals because everybody is looked after in their own right and no-one has to look after anyone else - there isn't any need for looking after them - like here we feed them and do all those things. You can be there in your dream state and sometimes they will come to you and ask you to visit them in dream state, but we don't understand it so we don't get there. It's very difficult because we may suddenly have a glimpse of the animals that we've known or it may not be an animal we think we've known, but we have known it some time and they will sometimes fleetingly visit you to almost ask you to visit them. Evidently some people have managed to get there in dream state but dismiss it afterwards."

I then asked about our seventeen year old dog Hattie who had become very senile and looked so unhappy these days. Christine said "I can't believe this is real - it's too ridiculous! I can now see Hattie beside the water on this patch of grass with all these flowers around and other animals, and she's rolling round the grass with her legs in the air and doing all of this..." (here I glanced at Hattie lying asleep on the floor with us in the lounge and her feet were twitching away and 'running' - so she was obviously somewhere!) "...now she's stood up and shaking herself and now looking towards him (the Spirit). Now he's saying to me *"You don't believe this do you?"*

"No I don't"

"Hattie's a friend from long, long ago. She's been down with you all many times because she has chosen to return. But first she flips back here any time that she wishes."

Christine "But she's so lively. So sort of.... And this smile again. And now he's saying *"You look at them"* - he's talking about animals in general now – *"and they look old and wizened as if they are unhappy with their life with you. They choose to stay the length of time they stay. But if something*

143

needs to be done to the physical body they can almost telepathically tell you".

Now I can see - for some time I've thought when do you make the decision to end an animal's life by the vet? It now appears that the seed can be sown in the mind by the animals themselves although you don't realise it and you think that it's you that's thought 'I'm going to have to make this decision'.

Now the Spirit is saying *"Sometimes we do it for you - sometimes you do it but life's like that."*

And "life was like that" several years before when my beloved Old English Sheepdog Panda, and Kim the lovely Collie, had to be 'put down' following a terrible illness they both had before I knew anything about healing, Dr Bach Flower Remedies or the fact that we all continue to live after leaving the body, of course.

I was devastated and hated to come back into the silent house,

walking anywhere but through the door to the unusual quietness within.

The pain of bereavement was with me for a very long time. I was still very raw and grieving for them both when they appeared to me as I described in the Lassie chapter where Panda showed me that Lassie would be alright. It was an amazing experience.

I often used to say when on the 'phone to a friend called Mary "Well I'm blessed!" when she told me something of great interest. She would reply "Indeed you are Marilyn!"

In a newspaper article in February 1993 I was very interested to read about some remarkable demonstrations of physical mediumship in the 1920s by a Polish gentleman named Franek Kluski a Warsaw bank manager. Specially arranged test sittings in university laboratories for members of the Polish Society for Psychical Research in Warsaw and the French Institut Metaphysique in Paris were arranged at which many animals made dramatic physical returns after their deaths. This remarkable man never worked in this field for gain, preferring to demonstrate his gifts for the benefit of science and research. Under very stringent conditions the most extraordinary animal manifestations took place.

One wonders why such things are not more well reported and people allowed to know about these truths that really no-one can die. We, the Spirit which inhabits these physical 'overcoats', move on to different wavelengths, frequencies, pulsations, perhaps of this very same world, occupying the very same space we are actually in now - like radio or television with hundreds of programmes all in the same space around us, but all different and completely separate and unknown to each other.

I have been given permission to quote from a wonderful book by an amazing nun, Sister Frances Banks - *'Frontiers of Revelation' "In seeking thus to integrate all emergent levels of reality, I found some satisfaction in a privately circulated book by a lecturer in mathematics called 'The Philosophy of Religion versus the Philosophy of Science 1935*(Albert Eagle) *lent to me by the late Mr Graham Moffat… and I find this passage carefully underlined:-*

If now we have another group of pulsating electrons, pulsating in a different period of time, these electrons would exert no average force on those of the former group. We can hence easily imagine that two totally distinct and independent worlds could exist in the same region of space and each would not only not interfere with the other in the slightest, but the beings in each would be perfectly unconscious and even incredulous of the existence of the other world.

I am reminded of my Church of England school's teachings and being made aware of the First Book of Corinthians talking of miracles and the gift of healing and to covet earnestly the best spiritual gifts.

And of 1 Corinthians chapter 15 verse 40: *There are also celestial bodies and bodies terrestrial but the glory of the celestial is one, and the glory of the terrestrial is another.*
And verse 44: It is sown a natural body, it is raised a spiritual body. There is natural body and there is spiritual body"
And verse 55: O death where is thy sting? O grave, where is thy victory?

It takes a very long time to start to find out what some of this means though. But what a treasure hunt!

Nipper - by Sheila & Ron King

Nipper is a rescue dog who came from hunting kennels. He did not have the aggression needed for hunting and was about to be destroyed when we took him as a pet at about eighteen months old.

In October 1995 he was attacked by two Boxer dogs whilst out for his morning walk. He lay on the ground twitching as if he had had a heart seizure.

Three weeks later he seemed to have some problem with his eyes. He was squinting in the light and the whites of his eyeballs had turned red. He had difficulty climbing steps and was bumping into obstructions.

We took Nipper straight to the vet and saw the senior partner of the practice. He thought the problem had been caused by cement dust and gave him eye ointment.

After a week of the treatment Nipper was completely blind and we happened to see the junior partner on our next visit to the vet. He altered the treatment to include eye drops plus water-reducing tablets and arranged for us to see an eye specialist at Tavistock in Devon.

The specialist explained that Nipper had suffered a trauma after being attacked and had built up fluid at the back of the eyes. The pressure of the fluid had detached the retinas and these were floating around loosely in the eyeballs. Luckily the tablets previously prescribed by our local vet were the correct ones and the specialist gave us additional tablets to try and relieve the pressure. It was hoped that eventually the fluid pressure would be reduced but there was no way to guarantee that the retinas would go back in place. The specialist warned us that we may have to take him to Newmarket, the only centre in this country at the time for animal laser treatment and there was no certainty that even this would succeed.

Our own vet in his note to the specialist stated "the owners have come to accept that their dog may be permanently blind"

By now we were getting desperate as it was difficult to exercise and feed Nipper and he was bumping into everything. He could not distinguish night from day and wanted to go out to walk at three in the morning.

We suddenly remembered that Marilyn used to treat animals years ago but assumed that she did not do this any more. However, we rang her and she invited us over to see her. She started healing immediately and after three sessions between visits to the vet the retinas had gone back in position and Nipper could see again.

The vet and the eye specialist were most surprised. When the vet had inspected his eyes a few days before the third session with Marilyn he used his pencil light and there was no reaction at all, just total blindness.

Before this time we had the impression that a healer helped a patient by triggering off some sort of self healing facility. In this case however, Nipper did not know what was happening to him but responded to Marilyn's healing completely.

We had given Marilyn a cross section drawing of the eye at the start of the session. It was a copy of the drawing done by the specialist when he explained the problem to us. From then on it was between Marilyn and Nipper. She did not have an easy task as he is a very lively dog and would not settle for long. At times he would go quiet and we realised Marilyn was getting through to him at these periods. We told the local vet afterwards where we had been and he was absolutely amazed.

Fliptod and Little Sunshine

On May 15th 1982 the following story of mine had appeared in the Western Evening Herald, a Plymouth daily paper with a very wide coverage in Devon and Cornwall. The article, as a letter, was unusually but beautifully illustrated with squirrel artwork, by someone in 'The Editor's Postbag'.

Early last year a friend brought a baby squirrel to me for help. I came to find that he was born without any eyes, later on, when investigating to find out why he hadn't opened them yet, after one of his bottle feeding sessions. But what a great sense of fun he had - and the gift of love and courage!

Young Fliptod started to get curious and discovered the huge Linden tree in our garden which became his home, after being weaned in our home and taken first to 'find his feet' in the aviary. One would never dream he had no sight, for he would race along the branches and come tearing down the trunk at the sound of my voice, to rush onto my out-stretched hand and arm.

He loved to cuddle in and be made a fuss of - he returned in full measure the love he was shown. Several times he was brought back from his wanderings by kind neighbours when he was off his familiar patch, and many people used to come and see and talk to our lovely little friend, Fliptod.

I became concerned when finding he began to gnaw wood - but then found it was only dead wood which he ever touched. Gnawing is essential to keep their teeth trimmed down - never did he use them on growing wood (although I realise this is unfortunately one of their 'bad' habits).

Fliptod did much more good than harm - he drew from people who came to meet him and talk to him, their love, admiration and compassion - and everyone left the better for the privilege of being with him for a while.

You see - many look on some species of animals and birds as pests - but each and every one of them has its own feelings, much as we humans have - in some cases, deeper than ours.

Unfortunately, some time later, young Fliptod died.

Fifteen years later, another little baby grey squirrel came into my hands. He had been hanging round his mother's neck being taken somewhere, when a cat pounced on them and he was dropped in panic. His mother never returned unfortunately, and I became his foster-mum and loved every minute of it, despite the fact my small Wild Bird and Animal Hospital / Sanctuary was by that time closed after some thirty years here.

I can't remember laughing so much, for years during our 'Squirrel Playtime' which we had several times a day. Never has a kitten or puppy played so happily or for so long as Little Sunshine! He would race up my leg and dash around under my clothes, popping his head out round my neck, or arm, or dash down my leg again, a leap onto my head would send me into fits of laughter as he'd pop down the neck of my blouse or up a sleeve to start a long mad game of hide-and-seek. Many friends and people coming for healing loved to come and see Little Sunshine's antics. However, with some people he would be aware of them coming up the garden path and would just freeze, watching them intently, but not moving a muscle. Nothing would coax him to play or move until I came out of the aviary and walked down the path with the disappointed visitors. It intrigued me - what was he aware of in them which made him so wary? Something he obviously understood about them, of which I was completely unaware. But one fine day, he was ready to return to the wild and I released him  from the aviary where he had lived so happily for some three months. I'd had a rope across the inside of the aviary for some time to get him used to climbing along it always upside down! Now I'd tied one to the outside across to the Linden tree and cut a hole in the wire netting beside it. With strict instructions to please return at any time, and for his bed and breakfast, he gingerly stepped out through the hole and onto the thick rope. Then he made his way to the tree, sat awhile on the branch and saw the tall pine trees behind him in the garden adjacent. Flying towards them he was lost to sight. Within a second or two there was a gurgled scream and silence.

I desperately called and called, hunting everywhere possible for him, knowing he would have come racing to me if he was able, but...silence.

By the next day it was evident he had been killed within a minute or two of his first freedom.

It was as though the sunshine had literally gone out of my life and I felt a very deep, anguished loss of a lovely, happy little friend, with whom I had shared 'prime time' every day because we both needed and enjoyed it so very much.

On the third day, I was again in the garden, by the aviary and questioning deeply 'WHY? WHY? in my mind, with the sadness that does not go away in states of bereavement.

Then the answer came, silently, deeply, but most assuredly. Little Sunshine was actually Fliptod who had returned to see me again, but this time with bright, shiny little happy eyes, wanting to SEE me, and Frederick, and his home where he had been raised so happily before, but as a blind friend. He saw the great Linden tree which had also been his home and all the many pigeons that came daily to feed - some of them having had to be hand-reared as he himself was, on both occasions, some of them brought in as patients by people who had found them ill or injured and in need of help and healing.

Having seen all these mysteries now, his mission was accomplished and he was freed to return Home again where we shall all meet up once more and wonder why we came to Earth in the first place. He certainly made the Earth plane a happier place - both times!

The Sunshine was switched on again in my mind, knowing that all was not in vain and that Fliptod and Little Sunshine were one and the same, with mission not only possible, but accomplished, bless him.

151

Henry Wilberforce Enderby

Before me as I write, is a thirty page letter from a lady in Surrey, written in 1992 about her cat, Henry, and which she wrote to record his story. Wendy fell in love with young Henry as soon as she saw him in a pet shop where she had gone to buy some rabbit food. The little tabby Siamese cross *'was a solitary figure with incredibly enormous ears and the most beautiful eyes.'* She paid thirty pounds for him and *'hurried away with him before anyone else could snap him up.'* Her husband Graham had always wanted a tabby and when she arrived home with him everyone was delighted and he was pronounced Henry Wilberforce.

Introductions were made to Ben, their Old English Sheepdog and Bun Bun, their beautiful large black rabbit who became the mother figure in young Henry's life. Henry was taken to their vet for a thorough check over, who thought he was quite special.

Several months later Bun Bun at the age of eleven, suffered a stroke and for three days could only flop to her litter tray, just wanting to lay quietly on her bed, with young Henry sitting quietly by her side as though he was willing her to get better. On the fourth day Bun Bun got to her feet and carried on as if nothing had happened, She lived on for another year after that. Henry was absolutely devastated by her death and became quite withdrawn. Wendy says that he grew up at that point as he has never been quite the same since.

A year later their beloved Old English Sheepdog Ben died during an operation to remove a brain tumour. Poor Henry, at only two years of age had lost both his family members, and Wendy and Graham took in another rescued Old English (they have four now - all rescued and all with problems, one blind, one deaf and two who have never been able to 'behave' themselves, as well as cats who needed homes, apart from other work they do which the average person could not possibly cope with - I think they are amazing folk). It was several months before Henry accepted Buster, Wendy saying that he looked at them as much to say 'You stupid people have brought the wrong dog back!"

Meanwhile they decided to try and find a soulmate for Henry, and Henrietta, a tortoiseshell kitten, joined the family. Very soon the pair were inseparable and the family was complete, or so they thought.....

The following year Wendy and Graham took in Tiggy, a one toothed black Siamese cross and Timsey, a blind grey tabby, both elderly, frail and doubly incontinent. Their ninety four year old owner had died and they had been left shut inside her house, starving. The RSPCA Inspector who gained access told them they were not suitable for re-homing, but the Enderbys decided to give them a home for the remaining weeks or months of their sad lives - which was already two and a half years at the time of Wendy's letter. The elderly cats were both very nervous, but extremely affectionate and quickly settled into the household, being accepted by all the four-legged friends. They went from strength to strength and were shown the utmost consideration by the other animals.

Then Barney, the delinquent black and white kitten came to stay awhile and has been there ever since.

Wendy writes that Sunday 8th September 1991 started off like any normal Sunday, but around half past four it was noticed that Henry had not been seen for awhile. She had spotted him several times that afternoon and each time she saw him kept thinking how beautiful he looked with the sun shining on his coat. By five o'clock they were beginning to get worried and began calling for him. Searching all the evening, she and Graham fell exhausted into bed around one in the morning, leaving the kitchen window open for him to come in, and going downstairs every so often to see if he'd arrived.

At six o'clock she rang the police and the emergency vet to report Henry's disappearance and went to a local building site to see the foreman to make enquiries before grudgingly going off to work. On her return and over the next few days Wendy rang all the vets in a thirty mile radius, all the police stations, the RSPCA, animal welfare groups, homes etc. The local radio station put out several appeals. Graham made large photocopies of a photograph of Henry showing his very distinctive markings, and with the caption "HAS ANYONE SEEN HENRY? They distributed these in pubs, shops and garages in five surrounding villages. She 'phoned the newspapers and was extremely fortunate to find their local newspaper sympathetic to their cause and who let them have a large double space with picture of Henry and caption. This they kindly repeated, free of charge, each week whenever space was available (doesn't that do one's heart good to know?)

HAS ANYONE SEEN HENRY?

LOST IN AREA SUNDAY 8th Sept
£100 OFFERED FOR HIS RECOVERY
PHONE 0483 772168

Armed with the original photo of Henry, Wendy & Graham began a daily trek around the neighbourhood, knocking on doors, asking if anyone had seen him - but no-one had. They returned home each night feeling desperate and disconsolate. Also disconsolate was Henrietta who crept into bed with them each night, a really dejected little figure huddled between them and their hearts went out to her.

Henry had been missing almost three weeks when they met Leonora. By now 'phone calls were coming in from far and wide, due to the widespread publicity -many people just wanting to give comfort and encouragement, which was much appreciated.

On Thursday 26th September a call came from two miles away - a possible sighting of Henry! Graham and Wendy spent the next two days and nights calling and searching and questioning everyone they met. On the Saturday afternoon they were directed to Leonora's house and she and her husband Jonathan turned out to be towers of strength to the desperate Enderbys, who were by now doubting they would ever see their beloved cat again. It was such a relief to find such deeply caring and helpful people. Leonora went out every night at midnight to check the nets on the local cricket pitch to make sure there were no hedgehogs trapped in them;

that night she spent another hour looking for Henry. She thought she saw him and they all spent the weekend trudging around in the pouring rain calling and listening. They abandoned their search at four o'clock on the Monday morning - and that was only because Wendy had to prepare a patient for a journey to Lourdes at four thirty.

They continued their search every evening and Leonora put food out and kept a night vigil.

Sunday 13th October started as painfully as any other day. It was now five weeks since Henry had disappeared and the possibility of seeing him again was getting more and more remote.

Then while out on a visiting round Wendy received a call out of the blue - it was from Graham. "I've got Henry - he got back as far as next door, but there is something wrong with him - he cannot stand and he is desperately thin." Graham rang the vet and Wendy rushed home as soon as she could, although she says she couldn't resist stopping on the way and telling a complete stranger "WE'VE GOT OUR CAT BACK!" she was so elated.

They rushed to the emergency surgery as their vet was off duty. Henry was certainly far from well - not only was he unable to stand, but was having convulsions every few minutes. He was also disorientated, dehydrated and had a sub-normal temperature. The duty vet was very concerned and said Henry may have picked up something toxic and that the situation was very grave. He gave him some injections and said they were to keep him warm, try to get some fluids into him and take him to their own vet first thing next morning. They returned home armed with a packet of Lactade, a syringe and a letter for their vet, only discovering later that Henry hadn't really been expected to survive the night, but the vet thought it would have been too cruel to separate them from him under all the circumstances.

The family were overjoyed to have Henry back again and though he was still having convulsions his relief to be home again was obvious. Dinner that evening was the first meal they had enjoyed in five weeks and their son said "Does this mean we can have Christmas now?" It took all evening spreading the wonderful news of the great return.

That night, their deeply loved cat went to bed stretched down the bed between them, Wendy and Graham hardly sleeping for fear of crushing the painfully thin and frail body. By morning he had regained his body heat and was admitted at their vet's clinic and put on a drip. They were told to ring later in the day. They rang in the afternoon and again in the evening but there had been little response to the treatment and it was decided he should be kept in overnight. They had the feeling that the nurses were being rather evasive and non-committal and their hearts filled with dread.

Their worst fears were confirmed next morning when their kindly vet 'phoned and said they had taken some blood tests etc. but that they, Wendy and Graham, must be very guarded as so far there had been no real change. The drip would be continued in the hopes that when Henry was fully re-hydrated the situation may improve.

Wendy wrote that the real bombshell came on the Wednesday morning when their vet telephoned to say that Henry had taken a turn for the worse, had started convulsions again during the night and had had to be sedated. The tests had shown that his central nervous system had broken down - either due to toxic poisoning or dehydration causing the metabolism to fuse. He had also developed a chest infection which they were treating with antibiotics. They were told to prepare themselves for the worst as there was a real possibility that Henry would not recover, as nothing could reverse the condition and indeed if he was not to enjoy some quality of life it may be kinder to put him to sleep. Wendy was absolutely stunned and horrified at the prospect of 'putting him out of his misery.' *"Henry must have used his last ounce of strength to get home to us - he trusted us to help him - we couldn't let him down. I knew he wanted to live I had seen it in his eyes - he was appealing for help and I knew he would put up a tremendous fight, so I said that everything that could be done must be done and no expense spared."*

She put the phone down and broke down, feeling so helpless. Then she suddenly remembered the book Leonora had loaned them on the previous Saturday - It was called *'Animals are Equal'* by Rebecca Hall, with a chapter on lost animals and how to will them to come home, which was quite amazing because it was the following day when Henry did come home. But she remembered the next chapter was on Animal Healing and although it was the last thing in the world that she would normally think of, she was desperate and thought she might at least find some comfort in reading it. She wrote that *'For the most part it featured an animal healer called Marilyn Preston and by the time I put the book down I knew I had found my answer,'*

She rang their vet and asked him how he felt about animal healers - he replied *"Anything is worth a try."*

'My next task was to find Marilyn - but where to start? The book was twelve years old. I rang Leonora as it was her friend Rebecca who had written the book, and to my delight she gave me Rebecca's telephone number. I rang with some trepidation - wouldn't she think it rather presumptuous of me to expect her to get in touch with Marilyn and at worst would she even know where Marilyn was after all this time? I need not have worried - not only did Rebecca know where she was, but provided me with her telephone number. I 'phoned Marilyn straight away. She asked me for all the details and assured me she would do her best - it was not necessary for her to see Henry - she would use absent healing.

I cannot describe the feeling of relief and the complete change of attitude that came over me after speaking with Marilyn. I just felt quietly confident that all would be well. Together with the family, we read again the chapter on healing and we adopted a really positive attitude - after all Henry didn't struggle home after all those weeks just to die; he is a very strong-minded cat and he certainly wasn't going to give up now.

The nurses were so surprised next morning to see Henry him curled up and looking so relaxed - up until then he had been hunched and rigid. Our vet was amazed at the improvement and could hardly believe his eyes. I telephoned Marilyn and said "I don't know what you are doing but whatever it is please keep doing it!"

157

Apparently I replied "We simply ask that the animal be lifted above his suffering, so that he can concentrate on getting well."

Graham and Wendy went to see Henry that afternoon and found a great difference from their visit the day before. Wendy lifted him up very gently, taking care not to disturb the drip tube in his paw - he settled into her arms and began to purr - something he did not normally do - he had never been a purry cat. They were overwhelmed and everyone was so delighted for them.

Henry steadily improved over the next few days and they kept in contact with me about his progress.

On the Saturday afternoon their vet told them that if they could get Henry to eat he would remove the drip and they could take him home. Everyone gathered round and they held their breath as Wendy offered him a small amount of the tinned red salmon they had taken in with them. '*He slowly began to eat, his jaws crunching painfully at the unfamiliar activity*', as she put it. Their wonderful vet smiled and begun to remove the drip tube - once again they took the cat home.

He was still far from well, but was now definitely on the road to recovery. Over the next few days he overcame many hurdles. His co-ordination improved and he began grooming himself and eating a normal diet. He learned to walk again and climb in and out of his basket and the litter tray, without having to be held steady, which was a great achievement. They noticed that he never attempted to try anything until he felt he was ready - he would sit and assess the situation first and if he felt it was too ambitious he would find an alternative way to go about it. For a long time he couldn't even get on or off a chair and they thought he would never manage the stairs again but over the months he had achieved everything and was still improving. They felt they were truly blessed to have their cat back and for all the wonderful kindnesses they had been shown *"We are truly privileged and we have only to look into Henry's eyes to know he feels it too..."*

We have kept in touch ever since and become good friends, though we have never met physically. This morning

Good Friday 2001, we received a lovely letter (and photographs) from Wendy, ending with *'Our love to you both and hope you have a Happy Easter, not that any of us can feel very happy with the terrible suffering and the senseless slaughter, due to this awful Foot and Mouth disease, of so many beautiful animals. This is indeed a very dark time.*

Henry sends his love - he is fourteen this month and very much the Boss. It is ten years now since his traumatic experience. Much love from us all - Wendy and Graham.'

On the 'phone this evening I asked Wendy if she would mind me writing this chapter and putting their surname - which she was very happy with, and she reminded me of another cat they telephoned me for help for, tests showed he was desperately ill with leukaemia. After absent healing further tests proved negative and the vet said *"What's this cat going to do next - walk on water?"* I wonder if he's tried it yet?

Piggy, Om and Little Miracle

Many years ago a baby bird had been brought to my door in an appalling state covered with oil and gasping for breath. Taking it in, I feared for its life as it was obviously on its last legs. However, I carefully washed it in warm, soapy water, after giving it some Dr. Edward Bach Rescue Remedy diluted in a little water. Keeping the shivering body warm until the shivers subsided, another dose of rescue Remedy brought some life back and the eyes brightened up - I think we stood a chance! Then I discovered it was a pigeon!

Piggy became our first pigeon, and what a friend she turned out to be! She immediately adopted me as her mother and followed me everywhere. Dennis had built the first aviary in the garden, a large one, for her but she much preferred being with us in the house. That must have been how The Wild Bird and Animal Sanctuary here really started.

She grew up into a really beautiful bird, though for a long time we thought she was a cock bird as she would fan her tail out, puff up her chest and circle me or anything for that matter, cooing for all she was worth. Pigeon fanciers came and asked to buy this wonderful 'cock bird' for their lofts as they would have liked to breed from 'him'. They were convinced she was a he!

Then she laid her first egg, in a pair of Dennis' socks I had on top of a box in the breakfast room. She did her best to hatch it but as she had never mated with another pigeon - she didn't like them as they were not her sort at all she reckoned -

160

it was of course infertile and finally Piggy gave up the effort and got on with her life - usually following me around.

Then came the difficult time, when she was persuaded to go out in the aviary, which had an open trap for her comings and goings. She found an ideal spotting place was on our roof where she could view all our comings and goings and began following me out shopping and down the town, flying from rooftop to rooftop, wall to wall then onto my shoulder and the pavement before me to do her little courting dance. I held my breath every time a car went past in case she flew into the road. Very often I would have to pick her up and bring her home, closing the trap door in the aviary to keep her in until I returned from shopping, where she would go frantic trying to get out again.

It got to the ridiculous stage where, when she was on the roof and I wanted to go shopping I would have to look to see which way she was facing, grab the shopping bag and creep out of the house the other way, stooping down, keeping close to the wall at the rear entrance or the little hedge which we had at the front garden in those days, almost crawling along to try to avoid her seeing me. People must have thought me absolutely crazy! And more often than not she would turn and spot me and we would have a right performance all over again, finally catching her and bringing her back home again.

One Saturday morning I thought I'd been clever and managed to get to the town centre. Being served in the local fruit shop, suddenly there was a screech of brakes and we rushed to the doorway to see what had happened.

There was Piggy, in the middle of Fore Street, tail fanned out, cooing round and round in the centre of the busy main street! I raced out of the shop, held up my hands to stop the rest of the traffic coming up the street, the other car having thankfully stopped as it could see the pigeon was not going to give way. Picking her up, my face as red as a beetroot, I tucked her under my arm and had to continue with the rest of my shopping which was extremely awkward. Later on, she was run over - twice- having flown down onto the roadway, with a car coming at a fast rate. Each time the car went right over her and she was left totally bewildered with not a coo left in her - little realising how lucky she had been each time.

Somehow we managed to survive some twelve years like this. Then one day whilst sitting in the breakfast room I noticed she was not feeling at all well. She began to take no notice of her food or drink and dropped her wings. This wasn't Piggy at all, what was wrong? I could find nothing at all to put my finger on and a couple of days later took her to our vet. He too was stumped until he finally realised she was egg-bound! We tried all ways to release the egg, but it finally broke and was unable to be fully extracted. Piggy went from bad to worse and died a few days later, amid my tears and sadness. Despite the shopping difficulties I missed her dreadfully.

Meantime several other pigeons had been brought in by people in various states of ill-health or injury. One of these was a racing pigeon who was in a bad way with a broken wing and other injuries. I did not expect him to survive but he made a good recovery in a remarkably short time and I traced his owner in Leicester. The owner of the bird, ring number GB81 WO9288 advised me to 'dispose' of him as he was no longer any use for racing. Obviously I could not 'dispose' of this young bird born that year of 1981. So he became a permanent guest for the next seventeen years! I reported his death in the British Homing World on 1st May 1998 with again much sadness. He too had been greatly admired by pigeon fanciers for breeding but I turned down all offers as he mated with an incoming patient in the second year and they became inseparable.

By this time Dennis had passed on and three years later I had married Frederick who had a lovely, specially designed pigeon loft built in our garden to house the growing number of pigeons who were brought in and homed here for the rest of their lives. The loft was always open so that they came and went as they pleased. The racer and his mate made first claim on the pigeon box nearest the door - the one on the top of the three-tiered rows of 'pigeon holes' so that whilst the hen nested in her box, the racer stood guard above her at all times, unless they were out flying the skies together.

Some years later, his mate, Fawny, went missing. By this time we had named the racer Om (Old Man) and each day we watched as he stood on one of our chimney pots, apparently watching the sky for his beloved mate's return. Each day I called to him to come in and at least have some food, but no, he took no food or drink for five days. I had put out advertisements for her return on our front, back and side entrances and also in the town. A pigeon, like swans, mates for life and Om was missing his mate terribly.

On the fifth evening, with Om still sitting on the chimney pot, I again tried to call him in. He suddenly started cooing around on the chimney pot, looking down into it, tail fanned out and getting quite excited. Suddenly the penny dropped, Fawny was down our chimney!

I raced into the house and pulled aside the various covers I had placed in front of all the fireplaces for the summer months. Finally I got to the back bedroom which had a large mirror fixed across the front of the fireplace. Ripping it away I shone the torch up the chimney, but no sign of any pigeon. Groping around as far as I could reach I discovered a second fireplace to the right of the main one and there was Fawny, covered in soot and grime but alive! With uplifted and thankful heart I carried her up into the pigeon loft, with Om in hot pursuit over my head. What a reunion they had! After which they both ate and drank for the first time in five days and nights. They were again inseparable.

Around that time I had a distressed call from a friend, Alison, who had a pair of fantail doves who were long time mates. One day a visiting van backed out of their drive and unfortunately killed the hen bird. Her mate stopped eating for several days and Alison was very concerned for him. She had been watching him from an upstairs window that morning, when she saw him fly down to the horse trough in the yard. He stayed for quite a while looking at the water, easily within drinking reach, then he suddenly dropped down into it, head under the water. She then realised he was not bringing his head up and ran downstairs and out to him - but he had drowned himself and put himself out of his torment. We had not realised before that birds commit suicide and it was extremely sad and thought provoking.

Came the day when I went into our pigeon loft as usual but to find several dead and dying pigeons lying on the floor. What on earth had done this? We thought that no predators could get into the loft. The others had flown and spent several days and nights sleeping out which they had never done before. All the birds had been patients - I dare not let them breed to increase the numbers and changed their eggs for china ones whenever they laid eggs, otherwise we would have ended up with hundreds of pigeons!

Gradually they returned to the loft, which we secured, we thought from any intruders. But next morning again devastation with two more dead birds, feathers everywhere, and some missing. One of those missing was Fawny and again Om was in distress and this time stood on the high SWEB wall adjoining our garden, sky watching for several days.

With no birds in the loft I set a cat trap with food and left it overnight. The following morning, there was the culprit - a black cat, very angry and frightened at being trapped. Putting him into another pen I advertised for the owner of this un doctored tom but no-one came forward and thankfully the Cats Protection League kindly agreed to take him, have him neutered and find a home for him.

I prayed every day that somehow, somewhere, Fawny was alive and hopefully recovering. Looking out of the bathroom window one day, suddenly there was a flutter and there was Fawny - beside her beloved Om! Later in the day they both flew onto the large building adjacent to our home and stayed there for another two days and nights. It was bitterly cold and I feared for them greatly. There was no way I could reach them. Finally they flew down onto our workshop roof and I was able to get a ladder and reach Fawny, by this time absolutely exhausted and ill after her trauma.

Bringing her indoors I gave her water, with rescue Remedy and some pigeon food but she was so weak she could barely pick it up so I gently force fed her. Meantime Om returned to his home in the loft and began to eat and drink. The few remaining pigeons also joined him there and we firmly secured the loft so that nothing could get in or out, just in case... During the daytime I took Fawny up into the loft to be with her mate, where he stood guard again over her, or moved into her little box with her, to be nearer.

A couple of days later Fawny breathed her last earthly breath and was gone, with Om nudging her with his beak trying to awaken her again. It was heart-breaking to see him so bereft as I took her body away and later buried it on the third day. I picked up a single feather she had dropped in her box.

On Fawny's death I tried to pacify Om and came into the house with a lump in my throat and in tears, carrying her fawn feather in my hand. I picked up the book *"A Course in Miracles"* and of all it's 1188 pages, opened it up at page 380 of the text to find to my amazement, the words *"Look not upon the little wall of shadows.."* *"This feather of a wish, this tiny illusion, this microscopic remnant of the belief in sin, is all that remains of what once seemed to be the world... How mighty can a little feather be before the great wings of truth?"*

As I read and held her feather I wondered how on earth this reading, out of the whole book, came at that particular time and sent out the wish that Fawny would now be happy, free and healthy again whilst she waited until it was Om's turn to join her. But that was not to be until eleven years later. He never mated with another bird and kept quietly to himself - I must have grieved for his loss as much as he did - all those years, watching him. And as I finished my letter printed in the British Homing World in 1998 "Om.. has only today left his physical body for higher skies" and hopefully to be rejoined with his beloved Fawny.

Another pair of pigeons were separated in the attack by the black cat, the hen being killed and her mate Grey being left. He too ate nothing nor would he drink, but stayed on the SWEB wall all day, coming in only when it was getting dark going straight to his mate's box. I grieved for his grief also and nothing would cheer me up in those sad, dark days.

Several days later, watching him sitting on the wall, from our bathroom window I cried for his distress and I prayed that God would take him and re-unite him with his dear companion. That night after he had returned to the loft and all the others were safely in, I locked up the loft, as now usual, making sure that not even a mouse could get in anywhere and nothing could get out.

Next morning I unlocked the door of the loft and immediately looked for Grey and Om, before glancing round at the other birds and before opening the trap to allow them their freedom for the day. But there was no Grey! He had totally disappeared! To this day it has remained a total mystery what happened to Grey - how did he de-materialise? It was absolutely impossible for him to have physically left the loft which had been his home for several years and to which he always returned, apart from the days and nights of the attacks. Had God heard my anxious prayer and called him Home?

Coming more up to date, a couple of years ago a dark pigeon landed in our garden in a terrible state. Both his legs were broken and two toes on each foot so he was unable to stand. Apart from that his feathering and skin were ripped from the whole of the front of his body, about two inches wide leaving a couple of ribs visible and all the flesh raw. What had caused such injuries I have no idea. It was late afternoon and I could not get him to the vet that day to have him 'put down' but I telephoned them to make an appointment for the following morning as I really thought there was no hope for him at all and it would be kinder to have him put out of his suffering as soon as possible.

But meantime he needed food and water but it was impossible for him to stand. So as a temporary measure I put splints on each leg and gently secured them, then making splints for his broken toes out of pipe cleaners, I taped these in place and watched as he stood up and took a few faltering steps! He drank deeply from a deep drinking bowl and began to eat and eat, and eat... I left him in his box in the house, making up my mind to keep the appointment next morning at the vet.

Next morning, on opening the box there was a bright-eyed, beautiful pigeon looking in my eyes with a great will to live, walking around his box with hardly a falter. He could cope at least with his feet and legs! I rang the vet and cancelled the appointment saying he was being given a chance. But how was his chest to be healed?

It was mild weather so I plastered the open chest, very gently with Dr Bach Rescue Cream - at least it would keep off the flies if nothing else! He went through this for a couple more days then I transferred him to the aviary and flight in the garden and tended him each day there. By the end of the week I removed the foot and leg splints and found to my joy that his toes and legs were perfectly healed! I was still praying about his chest.

About two weeks later, going into the aviary one morning I saw to my utter amazement that the pigeon's chest was not only fully healed but covered in perfect feathers! Shouting for Frederick we both looked at him in wonder - and named him Little Miracle, for that indeed was what it was.

Releasing him into the garden at feeding time for all the other pigeons who daily come, many of them ex patients, he readily joined them, his flock, and came back each day to feed. I always ring my pigeons who come in for treatment and healing and for over a year I proudly watched Little Miracle, red ringed on his left leg, return every day.

And Now.....

Days continue to be full with people and animals coming for healing.

The three weeks before Christmas we have learned to keep free of healing sessions as we send and receive some three hundred and fifty cards and letters on average - and that takes an awful lot of work until two or three every morning. A few friends have been absolutely marvellous and send postage stamps to cover most of these cards going out together with our Christmas letter which can be several pages long. It is quite a task every Christmas! Frederick would come back from the post saying "There's not many people down the town!" Well no there wouldn't be at 3am would there?

My dear old dad was taken to hospital, and passed out of his worn out physical body on Sunday 24th January 1999, just before his ninety-sixth birthday. I'd often talked about continuing life after what we term 'death' and he'd said he wished he could really believe it. Hence in the obituary in the local paper we'd added the words: "See! It's all true! Remember to look to the light!" followed by some words scribed on the east window of Paul Church, Cornwall where I was christened " And you will speed us onward with a cheer and wave beyond the stars that all is well" God Bless, dear Dad, see you! Our fondest love and blessings."

I am so thankful he 'comes through' a friend now and he is of course no longer blind but very well and happy and it has been amazing how he is aware of things here and tells us about it through Joy, quoting the exact words and phrases I have used talking to Frederick. He also has the pleasure of Thor, the swan's, company 'over there' in his new dimension of continuing and happier life.

Birds are still being brought in now and again although the 'hospital' has been closed for some years. Each one takes quite a time each day to care for and then eventually, hopefully release. Meantime some fifty or so pigeons come daily for their food, some of these are old patients who have never forgotten their sanctuary - some were hand reared here after folk had brought them to the door, some have been coming for many years.

Just on writing the foregoing I went up into the garden to give the pigeons their special food and was delighted to see Little Miracle back again, looking in tip top condition, legs and feet perfect and a smartly feathered chest, what a joy that was.

'Strappers' too often find their way here when they see the flock, and these lost racing pigeons will rest and stock up with food and water until they feel strong enough to continue their journey. We recently have had one in from Holland.

A few weeks ago, amid the pigeons who came to feed, one crash landed on the lawn, then staggered up on one leg. He allowed me to pick him up and examine his right leg. It was badly broken and his foot was paralysed, with toes curled under, quite dead and cold. Taking him indoors Frederick gently held him on the table whilst I felt the broken joint, moved the bones into the right position and fixed it firmly with Micropore.

Then we had a session on his paralysed foot and toes, spreading his three forward toes out in front, the rear one then extending backwards, and bending the ever helpful pipe cleaner to fit this now correct position, taping it with micropore. The pigeon was an ideal patient and did not struggle throughout this procedure or the following healing session on his leg, foot and toes. He settled down in a large wire fronted box in the aviary, very contentedly, moving only to eat and drink. By the third day I was impressed to take off the micropore and the pipe cleaner on his foot and toes - they were healed beautifully! Three days later the micropore on the pigeon's leg was removed - and there was a beautifully healed bird walking quite normally and happily again! Placing the blue ring on the other leg I then released him from the aviary and "Feathers" is usually the first one back every day to feed with the others now. (He's called that because his legs are covered with small feathers).

When one gets to know individual birds and animals a bond forms which is very personal and warm and one sees them in a different light then - like the brilliant scientist to

169

whom we on the Earth plane owe so very much - Dr. Nikola Tesla. His is a name few people recognise.

When I first heard of it several years ago I was immediately agog with excitement as something within recognised it with deep pleasure, though why I had no idea at the time. Looking out for books about this man, I was not disappointed in what came to light!

Replying to a published article in the Western Morning News about '...the work of telecommunications genius, Guglielmo Marconi.' My published reply in that newspaper dated 21st March 2001 reads:

"CHALLENGING MARCONI AS FOUNDER OF RADIO"
Having read your story 'Marconi Centre wins vital funding', I feel that it is important to set the record straight about the history of radio, and to celebrate the work of telecommunications genius Nikola Tesla. I then quoted James Coates from the Chicago Tribune of Sunday 10th August 1986 in which he states that two years before Marconi demonstrated his wireless radio transmission, Tesla, performed an identical feat at the 1893 World's Fair in Chicago. On 21st June 1943, in the case of Marconi Wireless Telegraph Co. versus the United States, the Supreme Court ruled that Tesla's radio patents had pre-dated those of the Italian genius....

From a very early age, Dr Tesla had many amazing spiritual gifts about which he wrote in part of his life story. When, at eight years of age he realised his character was weak and vacillating, he thought deeply about it, *'until all at once, there came a tremendous change which altered the course of my whole existence.'* Dormant powers of will were awakened and he began to practice self control with vigorous mental exercises until it became second nature. He passed through the most dreadful diseases, being at the point of death at times, (later becoming fanatical about cleanliness to an extraordinary degree.)

Nikola Tesla's parents then had to move from beautiful countryside to the city of Gospic and he was devastated having to part from their pigeons, chickens, sheep and *'magnificent flock of geese which used to rise to the clouds in the morning and return from the feeding grounds at sundown in battle formation.'*

When he was gone forty and whilst carrying out his electrical experiments in Colorado, he could hear very distinctly thunderclaps at a distance of five hundred and fifty miles, the ticking of a watch three rooms away; a fly alighting on a table in the room would cause a dull thud in his ear; the whistle of a locomotive twenty or thirty miles away made the bench or chair on which he sat, vibrate so strongly that the pain was unbearable, and he had to support his bed on rubber cushions to get any rest at all. But he later became unbelievably strong, working every day of his long life, often twenty hours a day and *'had so much energy to spare.'*

Having designed a multitude of machines and instruments and invented so many things which make our life so much more advanced today both in the home and in hospitals, he continued to work incessantly, explaining: *'The gift of mental power comes from God, Divine Being, and if we concentrate our minds on that truth we become in tune with this great power.'*

But the other side of this brilliant man was his great love of pigeons. Every day he would walk the streets feeding 'his' birds and should he be too busy, he would pay his staff to do so. He would look for the injured birds and take them back to his rooms at whatever hotel he was living in at the time to give them healing until they were well enough to fly off again. When he started this practice he would be dressed in the height of fashion and some of the worlds most famous figures would often be seen in his company, joining him in feeding his feathered friends; and despite his need for total cleanliness, he was most happy to allow the pigeons to alight on him wherever they could find a footing. He was never ever concerned about any possible disease they may be disputed to carry - only from humans, with whom he could barely bring himself to shake hands in case they transferred disease to him, as with his childhood illnesses, which had nearly killed him several times.

In John J O'Neill's book *"Prodigal Genius - The Life of Nikola Tesla - Inventor Extraordinary"* O'Neill, whose attributes take up a whole page, including science editor of the New York Herald tribune for several years, and a Pulitzer Prize winner, tells of his great friendship with the genius. He referred to Dr Tesla as a "scientific superman" who had made his first million before he was forty, yet gave up his royalties on his most profitable invention to aid a friend, refused to accept the Nobel Prize, and died almost in poverty.

The book tells us how difficult it was for anyone to understand why this amazing scientist who worked twice as many hours as the average individual, should spend time feeding flocks of pigeons. One of these birds was a white female with touches of light grey on her wings - on the tips. With her, Nikola Tesla had a tremendous bond and went to great lengths to make sure she was well cared for. When he was very ill and had to remain in his office he employed a housekeeper to feed and water her each day in his hotel room until he was able to get there himself.

Some months later, he telephoned his secretary to say he was alright, but his pigeon was ill and he had to remain with her, which he did for several days. He was devastated when she died the following year and the light went out of his life, yet he knew she continued to live on and that he would rejoin her after his physical death, of course, as is told in much more detail in Margaret Storm's book *Return of the Dove*- Dedicated to Nikola Tesla, this book provides the scientific answer to the great spiritual needs of today's world.

John O'Neill tells in his book of an amazing conversation with Dr Tesla, in the company of a friend relating the love story of Tesla's life. He stated he had been feeding pigeons, thousands of them, for years. One of these was a beautiful pure white bird with light grey wing tips. Wherever he was the White Dove would always find him and they loved each other deeply - *"That pigeon was the joy of my life! If she needed me, nothing else mattered. As long as I had her, there was a purpose in my life."*

The elegant, handsome scientist then told his two listeners that one night, lying in bed in the dark, solving problems as he usually did then, the love of his life flew in through the open window (he always kept his window open for the birds) and stood on his desk. He knew that she had something very important to tell him (he had always been telepathic) - he got out of bed and went to her. She told him she was dying. *"And then, as I got her message, there came a light from her eyes - powerful beams of light... It was a real light, a powerful, dazzling, blinding light, a light more intense than I had ever produced by the most powerful lamps in my laboratory.*

"When that pigeon died, something went out of my life. Up to that time I knew with certainty that I would complete my work, no matter how ambitious my program, but when that something went out of my life I knew my life's work was finished. Yes, I have fed pigeons for years, I continue to feed them, thousands of them, for after all who can tell ".

Earlier this year I read that chapter from Mr O'Neill's book to Frederick. Being deeply moved by it I asked Dr Tesla if he could bring us some sort of proof of his presence which we have been told, on occasions, is often here with us.

The following morning Frederick went up into the garden to feed the pigeons, assembled for their meal and he came down a minute later to tell me a new pigeon had joined the flock - a pure White Dove, with grey wing tips!! I hurried up to see for myself and she really was a beautiful bird, whom we had never seen before. She came a few times but since then has not returned. "But after all, who can tell…?"

—— · ——

Acknowledgements

p21,24,26   *Lychgate – Entrance to the Path* Air Chief Marshal Lord Dowding, Rider and Co, London, 1945.

p21,27   *The Dark Star* Air Chief Marshal Lord Dowding
Museum Press Ltd, London, 1951

p21   *Many Mansions* Air Chief Marshal Lord Dowding, 1944

p68   *The Medical Discoveries of Edward Bach Physician*
Nora Weeks, C.W Daniel Co. Ltd, London 1973

p71   *Reunions* Raymond Moody Villard, New York, 1993

p71   *Life and Teaching of the Masters of the FarEast*
Baird T Spalding, DeVorss & Co, Camarillo, 1924

p72   *More Wisdom of Silver Birch,* ed. Sylvia Barbanell, Spiritualist Press, London, 1955 3rd imp.

p74, 120,122 & 157
Animals are Equal, Rebecca Hall, Wildwood House, London 1980, and later by Rider Books

p99   *The Celestine Prophecy,* James Redfield, Warner Books, 1993

p99, 112,165   *A Course in Miracles*, Helen Schucman, Foundation for inner Peace, Mill Valley CA, USA, 1992

p145   *ThePhilosophy of Religion Versus The Philosophy of Science: An Exposure of the Worthlessness and absurdity of Some Conventional Conclusions of Modern Science,* Albert Eagle, privately printed, Manchester, 1935

p145	*Frontiers of Revelation- an Empirical Study in the Psychology of Psychic and Spiritual Experience*, Frances Banks, Max Parrish, London, 1962
p171	*Prodigal Genius. The Life of Nikola Tesla Inventor Extraordinary,* John J O'Neill, Neville Spearman, London, 1968
p172	*Return of the Dove*, Margaret Storm Publications, Baltimore, 1959

The above publications were identified as still being available for sale through **www.abebooks.com**